AF608192

PREJUDICIAL ATTEMPTS IN PENDING LITIGATION

This dissertation was approved by the Very Rev. John Rogg Schmidt, J.C.D., LL.B., Professor of Canon Law, as director, and by the Rt. Rev. Edward Roelker, S.T.D., J.C.D., and the Rev. Romaeus O'Brien, O.Carm., J.C.D., as readers.

THE CATHOLIC UNIVERSITY OF AMERICA
CANON LAW STUDIES
No. 379

Prejudicial Attempts in Pending Litigation

A HISTORICAL SYNOPSIS AND A COMMENTARY

A DISSERTATION
SUBMITTED TO THE FACULTY OF THE SCHOOL OF CANON LAW
OF THE CATHOLIC UNIVERSITY OF AMERICA IN PARTIAL
FULFILLMENT OF THE REQUIREMENTS FOR THE
DEGREE OF DOCTOR OF CANON LAW

BY THE
REV. JOHN P. DUNNIVAN, A.B., J.C.L.
Priest of the Archdiocese of Kansas City
in Kansas

THE CATHOLIC UNIVERSITY OF AMERICA PRESS
WASHINGTON, D.C.
1960

Nihil Obstat:
JOANNES ROGG SCHMIDT, J.C.D.
Censor Deputatus
Washingtonii, D.C. die 7a maii 1957

Imprimatur:
✠ EDUARDUS J. HUNKELER, D.D., LL.D.
Archiepiscopus Kansanopolitanus in Kansas

Kansanopoli, die 9a septembris 1959

Printed by The Abbey Press, St. Meinrad, Indiana, U.S.A.

MARIAE
OMNIUM CORDIUM
REGINAE

FOREWORD

In this dissertation the purpose of the writer is to examine the judicial significance of prejudicial attempts (*attentata*) during the course of a trial or an appeal. The considerations given to the nature, elements, solution and revocation of prejudicial attempts committed by a judge or the litigants will, it is hoped, clarify the term *attentatum* somewhat for those who are appointed to protect the rights of the litigants in a trial. Since it is only just that a party should have a means or a remedy whereby he may obtain redress for injuries inflicted upon himself, such a remedy is provided for by the law, even though the injury is not the principal question under consideration, but nevertheless flows from it in some way.

It is not intended in the dissertation to give an exhaustive treatment of all the various way in which a prejudicial attempt can be committed during a trial or an appeal. To do so would necessitate much more research into all the possible acts which could be construed as effecting prejudice to the litigants. Such prolonged research is not necessary either to gain a general view of the historical development of the law with reference to attempts, which may occur during the pending litigation, or to illustrate the principles found in the Code as pertaining to prejudicial attempts.

The first portion of the Historical Synopsis will be devoted to an examination of the rule of law, *ut lite pendente nihil innovetur,* which underlies the whole consideration of prejudicial attempts, and to which the subject matter regarding attempts corresponds in the Decretals of Gregory IX. In the second part of this synopsis, only the historical development of the elements of prejudicial attempts, which are included in the concept of *attentata* as found in the present Code of Canon Law, will be discussed.

In the Canonical Commentary, the nature of the present law which governs the incidental question of prejudicial attempts is inspected, especially in regard to the beginning and termination of the pending of the litigation. The precise determination of the *litis pendentia* was perhaps the most elusive problem confronted by the writer. The beginning of the pending litigation is specifically defined by law and adequately discussed by the various authors. The termination of this juridical entity, however, is neither expressly defined by any single canon, as is its inception, nor is it specifically determined to any satisfication by the authors themselves. For this reason a detailed discussion on the pending of the litigation was thought to be imperative at the outset.

Mention has already been made as to the inadvisability of discussing every act which might constitute a prejudicial attempt. Though this is so, it was deemed necessary to review many elements of canonical procedure, in order that the matter of prejudicial attempts could be better appreciated as a whole. To this end, efforts were made to consider the requisites which an act must possess before it can be designated as an *attentatum*. These requisites or conditions provide the general outline for the fourth chapter. The basis for the final chapter is the nullity of attempts, the action granted against them, and the mode of procedure employed to declare this nullity.

The writer welcomes this occasion to express his sincere gratitude to His Excellency, the Most Reverend Edward J. Hunkeler, D.D., Archbishop of Kansas City in Kansas, for the opportunity of graduate study in Canon Law at the Catholic University of America. He also wishes to thank the members of the Faculty of the School of Canon Law, his classmates at the University, and all others whose scholarly guidance, helpful suggestions, and kind encouragement have made this dissertation possible.

TABLE OF CONTENTS

PART I
HISTORICAL SYNOPSIS

CHAPTER I

HISTORICAL DEVELOPMENT OF LEGISLATION AGAINST PREJUDICIAL ATTEMPTS BEFORE GREGORY IX

Article 1. Introductory Notions

The Church, constituted by Christ as a perfect society, from its very beginning has legislated for its members in matters both spiritual and temporal. This fact is proved from sacred history. For we read that St. Paul, the great Apostle to the Gentiles, forbade certain Christians of Corinth to cite their brethren before secular courts.[1] St. Paul's protest expressed the conviction that the Church alone had exclusive competence to take cognizance of the various problems that would arise among the Church's members. It was with this understanding and firm belief that Christians of all times have guided their actions. Time and again bishops have been called upon to settle claims between individuals, between individuals and communities.[2]

Ever since its beginning the Church has constantly asserted its exclusive right and power in matters that are purely spiirtual. The Church always reserved to itself the right of adjudicating causes that arose among the clergy themselves or in which they were involved. This right of clerics to have their causes tried in ecclesiastical courts is termed the *privilegium fori.* This is still true, even though the Church, for reasons of peace and harmony, has allowed these causes to be taken into the secular courts in such places as the United States, either because it has tacitly tolerated such a procedure or expressly agreed to it.

Finally, the Church has always claimed as its exclusive right the adjudication not only of spiritual causes and of

[1] I Cor. VI, 1-9.

[2] Abbo-Hannan, *The Sacred Canons* (2 vols., St. Louis: B. Herder Book Co., 1952), II, 755.

temporal causes that are inseparably connected with the spiritual, but even of those temporal causes which are in any way connected with the spiritual.[3]

During the course of a trial, the principal cause is examined by the judge. Proofs by the plaintiff are presented to substantiate his allegations or assertions which were made to the tribunal. The defendant, if he denies these assertions, must present his proofs to the tribunal. The cause is closed by a definitive sentence, becoming irrevocably adjudged (*res iudicata*). Within the framework of a trial oftentimes questions will arise which are derived from the principal cause. They, as it were, receive their being from the main consideration at hand. Such questions are called incidental questions. The treatment of prejudicial attempts falls within this category. Though incidental questions of this nature are not contained in the bill of complaint (*libellus*), nonetheless their nature is such that they must be resolved before the principal cause, unless the judge deems it more advantageous to postpone their solution and to include them in the solution of the principal cause itself.

In the judicial sense *attentare* means to do something contrary to a prohibition. This prohibition in a judicial matter can be made *a iure* (prohibition of law or general prohibition) or *ab homine* (prohibition of man or special prohibition). Thus, in a trial or in an appeal, if the judge

[3] Beste, *Introductio in Codicem* (3. ed., Collegeville, Minn., 1946), p. 772 (hereafter cited as *Introductio*). "Eventually Roman law itself invested bishops with judicial competence not only for those cases involving ecclesiastical matters, but also, at the choice of the parties, for those involving purely secular matters. The judgment of the bishop was rendered after a rather simple procedure based almost entirely on the principles of the natural law, among the acts of which the chief were the following: the right of the accused to be heard, the presumption of his innocence until his guilt had been proved beyond the shadow of a doubt, his right to appeal, and a punishment proportionate to his guilt."—Abbo-Hannan, *The Sacred Canons*, II, 755. Ottaviani, *Institutiones Iuris Publici Ecclesiastici*) 3. ed., 2 vols., Civitate Vaticana: Typis Polyglottis Vaticanis, 1947-1948), I, 257-293.

imposes certain prohibitions, the law forbids any violation of them. When a prohibition has been imposed (whether a general or a special prohibition), the litigants of a cause possess the right that nothing prejudicial should be done against them. This right can be violated either by the parties or by the judge. Any violation of this right of the parties is called a prejudicial attempt (*attentatum*).[4]

In the first part of this thesis it will be the endeavor of the writer to trace the development of the general rule of law under which the prohibition against prejudicial attempts during pending litigation will come: *Ut lite pendente nihil innovetur.*

ARTICLE 2. THE *Decretum Gratiani*

Gratian ushered in the period of Canon Law called the *Ius Novum.* It is his work that marked an important innovation in the field of ecclesiastical law. Gratian's work was the final and most comprehensive compilation of canon law from the time of the Pseudo-Apostolic works to Innocent II († 1142). His efforts were superior because of the extended number of the canons and the quality of his work. To him we attribute the final crystallization of the ancient canon law.[5]

Pope Gelasius (492-496) by the following decretal as incorporated in the *Decretum Gratiani* introduced into ecclesiastical law the prohibition against prejudicial attempts during a trial.

> Quia res in litigio posita in nullam transferri potest omnino personam, donec legitime cognitionis eventu, cui potius debeatur, iudiciaria disceptione possit agnosci ex eadem re quispiam non sinatur exigere pensiones, sed in eodem statu re eadem posita, in quo videtur (sicut dictum est) ante constituta, quisquis sibi putat quippiam posse con-

[4] Wernz-Vidal, *Ius Canonicum* (7 vols. in 8, Romae: Apud Universitatis Gregorianae, 1923-1938), VI, 519.

[5] Van Hove, *Commentarium Lovaniense in Codicem Iuris Canonici, Prolegomena ad Codicem Iuris Canonici* (editio altera, Mechliniae-Romae, 1945), I, 339 (hereafter cited as *Prolegomena*).

> petere, iuridico pulset examine, praeiudiciis omnibus inde submotis.[6]

This decretal in the *Decretum Gratiani* is the reply of Pope Gelasius to the litigants in a cause which had been presented to him. The defendant in the litigation had possession of the object of controversy (*res litigiosa*). It was asked whether the plaintiff could demand recompense. Gelasius replied that this could not be done before the cause was concluded by way of a definitive sentence. The object of controversy was to be retained by the defendant until its rightful owner was determined. If, however, during the trial any prejudicial acts occurred, they were null and void. The object of controversy was to be restored to the status which it had at the beginning of the trial.

The *Glossa* in a discussion of the term *res litigiosa* stated that it was anything whose dominion was controverted either in a quasi cause between the plaintiff and possessor, in a judiciary *conventio,* or in a petition to a superior.[7] If the object of controversy was alienated, the act was null.[8]

[6] C. 50, C. XI, q. 1. Jaffé, *Regesta Pontificium Romanorum ab condita Ecclesia ad annum post Christum natum MCXCVIII* (editio altera, correctam et auctam auspiciis G. Wattenbach curaverunt F. Kaltenbrunner, P. Ewald, S. Loewenfeld, 2 vols., Lipsiae, 1885-1888), n. 712 (hereafter cited as *Regesta*); Mansi, *Sacrorum Conciliorum Nova et Amplissima Collectio* (53 vols., Paris-Leipzig-Arnhem, 1901-1927), VIII, 131; Migne, *Patrologiae Cursus Completus, Series Latina* (221 vols., Paris, 1844-1855), LIX, col. 146 (hereafter cited as *MPL*).

[7] *Glossa Ordinaria,* ad c. 50, C. XI, s.v. *in litigio*: "Res dicitur litigosa, de cuius domino, vel quasi causa vertitur inter petitorem et possessorum, vel iudiciaria conventione, vel precibus principi oblatis, et per eum adversario cognitis." Wernz (*Ius Decretalium* [6 vols., Vols. I-IV, Romae et Prati, 1905-1913], V, p. 427) in citing his *fontes* for lib. II, tit. 16, of the Decretals of Gregory IX, gave two references to the *Decretum Gratiani* which appear to be a misprint, namely, c. 20, C. XI, q. 1; c. 2, C. XVI, q. 1.

[8] *Glossa Ordinaria,* ad c. 50, C. XI, q. 1, s.v. *quia res*: "Qui autem rem litigiosam alienat, et alienatio nulla est." Then various exceptions to this rule were given: "In casibus tamen licite alienatur res litigiosa, scilicet ex causa dotis, vel transactionis, vel donationis propter, nuptias,vel ex causa legati, vel divisionis rerum haereditariarum."

Guido De Bayso († 1313) spoke at some length of the necessity of restoring the object of controversy to its original status. He gave as a rule that, during the pending litigation, there were to be no innovations before the definitive sentence; furtherfore, the possessor of the object of controversy was to be given the protection of the law until the definitive sentence was imposed.[9]

Among the various ways in which a person's right in regard to the object of controversy could be prejudiced, Guido listed these four: 1) sale, 2) alienation, 3) donation, and 4) petitioning for a privilege or rescript to retain the object of controversy in one's possession.[10]

Rufinus († c. 1190) stated that the alienation of the litigious object was so forbidden that a person, if he had purchased such an object and knew that it had been alienated, was not entitled to the return of the price which he paid. If any contract was entered into *ex donatione,* it was to be revoked as null.[11]

Summa Parisiensis, ad c. 50, C. XI, q. 1, s.v. *quia res,* stated: "Hoc de causa intelligendum est quae in neutrius litigantium est possessione; vel quando possessor appellat, scilicet quasdam res sequestrat, ut habuimus ex legibus in secunda causa. Vel possumus breviter dicere quod res in litigio posita non debet vendi vel donari quousque evincatur ab alterutra." C. (8.37) 4.

[9] *Rosarium seu in Decretarum Volumen Commentaria* (Venetiis, 1577), ad c. 50, C. XI, q. 1, s.v. *quia res* (hereafter cited as *Rosarium*).

[10] *Rosarium,* ad c. 50, C. XI, q. 1, s.v. *praeiudiciis*: "Omnibus illis submotis et cassatis. Et nullum nocumentum vel praeiudicium alteri parti facientibus. Sed pendente lite circa rem litigiosam ab illa parte aliqua facta sunt contra ius, scilicet, vendendo vel alienando vel donando vel privilegium sive rescriptum ut liceat sibi retineri impetrando."

[11] *Die* SUMMA DECRETORUM (herausgregeben von H. Singer, Paderborn: F. Schöningh, 1902), ad c. 50, C. XI, q. 1, s.v. *quia res*: "Prohibetur autem alienatio rei litigiosae adeo, ut emptor qui sciens emit pretium amittat; qui autem ex donatione eam accepit, in aestimatione tertiae partis puniatur, contratu in irritum revocando."

CHAPTER II

HISTORICAL DEVELOPMENT OF THE LAW, *UT LITE PENDENTE NIHIL INNOVETUR,* FROM GREGORY IX TO THE COUNCIL OF TRENT (1545-1563)

ARTICLE 1. DECRETALS OF GREGORY IX

Because of the number of compilations made of papal decretals after the time of Gratian, a considerable amount of confusion arose. It was entirely unsatisfactory to go over the same matter five times.[1] There resulted frequent misquotations and misleading references. Occasionally private attempts were made to unite the five compilations, but without noteworthy success.

Pope Gregory IX (1227-1240), shortly after his accession to the papal throne, appointed Raymond of Pennafort, a Dominican, to the task of making a comprehensive collection of decretal law in the year 1230. St. Raymond completed this undertaking in about fuor years' time. With the Bull *Rex Pacificus,* issued by Gregory IX on September 5, 1234, the collection was introduced to use.

Three effects of the pending of the litigation (*litis pendentia*) are brought out in the five decretals of lib. II, tit. 16, in the Decretals of Gregory IX: 1) a party may not request a rescript in prejudice of the other litigant, unless mention of the pending litigation is made in the petition.[2] 2) A party shall not be deprived of a possession, even though there be question of matrimony, until the cause is finished.[3]

[1] Cf. Van Hove, *Prolegomena,* p. 355, for a detailed history of the *Quinque Compilationes Antiquae.*

[2] C. 1, X, *ut lite pendente nihil innovetur,* II, 16. C. 5, X, *ut lite pendente, etc.,* II, 16; Potthast, *Regesta Pontificium inde ab anno post Christum natum MCXCVIII ad annum MCCCIV* (2 vols., Berolini, 1874-1875), n. 7753 (hereafter cited as *Regesta*).

[3] C. 2, X, *ut lite pendente nihil innovetur,* II, 16; Jaffé, *Regesta,* n. 17649; Mansi, XXII, 638; *MPL,* CCVI, col. 1255.

3) The object of controversy cannot be alienated. If alienation does take place, the litigious object must be restored, or its equivalent substituted.[4] Such alienation changes the status of the object of controversy, and prejudices the other litigant.

ARTICLE 2. *Liber Sextus* OF BONIFACE VIII

The next important compilation of papal decretals after that of Gregory IX was the work of three persons: a) Gulielmus de Mandagato († 1323), the Archbishop of Embrum, b) Berengarius Fredoli († 1321), the Bishop of Béziers, and c) Richardus Petronius de Senis († 1314), Vice-Chancellor of the Roman Church. This collection was made at the command of Pope Boniface VIII (1294-1303). The compilation was given to the world in 1298 with the Bull *Sacrosancta.* It was called the *Liber Sextus Decretalium* because it was looked upon as an addition to the decretals of Gregory IX.[5]

In the *Liber Sextus* the title, *ut lite pendente nihil innovetur,* has two decretals.[6] The question that is discussed in these decretals treated of benefices: what should be done, if, during a pending cause, any innovation is made when benefices are the object of controversy.

The first decretal is the reply of Boniface VIII in a cause in which two persons claimed that they had been elected to a vacant benefice. Boniface decreed that there could be no new election until the controversy over the first election was adjudicated. This would be true, even though one of the litigants should die, renounce any right in the controversy that he might possess, or be excluded from the cause. If, however, another election were held while the cause was

[4] C. 3, X, *ut lite pendente etc.,* II, 16; Potthast, *Regesta,* n. 879; c. 4, X, *ut lite pendente etc.,* II, 16.

[5] Van Hove, *Prolegomena,* pp. 363-365.

[6] C. 1, 2, *ut lite pendente etc.,* II, 8, in VI°.

pending, such an election would be null *ipso iure;* it would be a prejudicial attempt.[7]

The reasoning followed in this decision is this: even though one of the litigants may have died, etc., nevertheless, the benefice does not cease to be a litigious matter. Since a doubt remained whether or not this person actually had any right to the benefice, a new election had to be postponed until the controversy was definitely settled. Otherwise, one of the litigants would be deprived of his lawful right.

The Glossator singles out the following as the principal effect of this decretal: no election may be held for the filling of a vacant benefice which is already the object of controversy. Once it is proved that the person who died, or who had renounced his right in the matter, or who had been excluded from resorting to judicial action, had no right to the benefice, a new election could then be held.[8]

In a comparison made between the two decretals in this title of the *Liber Sextus,* little difference is found to exist between the two. In the first decretal, neither of the litigants was in possession of the benefice which had become the object of controversy. In the second decretal, one of the parties had already gained possession of the benefice, while the other petitioned the court to settle the controversy. Boniface VIII decreed once again in this second cause that no new election could be held until the controversy over the benefice had been adjudicated and carried to completion by the court.[9]

The Glossator noted in his consideration of the cause that the principal effect of this second decretal was the following: if the defendant should die, while the cause is being adjudicated, the ordinary may not allow another elec-

[7] C. 1, *ut lite pendente nihil innovetur,* II, 8, in VI°: "Statuimus ut... ad electionem aliam, lite super electione superstitis electi pendente, nullatenus procedatur; alias attentata contra hoc electio ipso iure viribus non subsistit."

[8] *Glossa Ordinaria,* ad c. 1, *ut lite pendente* etc., II, 8, in VI°.

[9] C. 2, *ut lite pendente nihil innovetur,* II, 8, in VI°.

tion, and thereupon substitute another person in the place of the defendant, unless it was possible for him to have done so while the defendant was still alive.[10]

ARTICLE 3. CONSTITUTION OF CLEMENT V

At the command of Clement V (1305-1314) another book or compilation was prepared. Thus it came to be known as the *Constitutiones Clementinae* or the *Liber Septimus*. It was of a supplementary nature. By his decree the Pope ordered that it should be authentic once the universities had received it. But it was only after he had died and his successor, John XXII (1316-1334), came to the papal throne that it was actually sent to the universities in the year 1317. The Constitutions were arranged according to the subject matter of the *Liber Sextus* of Boniface VIII.[11]

Pope Clement issued the first decretal of the fifth title, *ut lite pendente nihil innovetur,* in his *Liber Septimus* about two years after it had been enacted in the Council of Vienne (1312). In it he decreed that the following rules were to be observed when litigation is pending in regard to a benefice and one or both of the litigants should die: 1) if the two litigants belong to the Roman Curia at the time of their death, the conferment of the benefice belongs to the Supreme Pontiff. Moreover, when only one of the litigants belongs to the Roman Curia but is in possession of the benefice at the time of his death, the Roman Pontiff will confer the benefice. The Pope will also make the conferment, if only one of the litigants belonged to the Roman Curia at the moment of his death, even though neither of the parties was in possession of the benefice. Finally, when there was proof that the benefice belonged to a cleric not in the Roman Curia at the time of his death, the Ordinary was to confer the benefice. 2) If only one of the parties died and the

[11] Van Hove, *Prolegomena,* pp. 365 f. Abbo-Hannan, *The Sacred Canons,* I, p. XVIII.

[10] *Glossa Ordinaria,* ad c. 2, *ut lite pendente etc.,* II, 8, in VI°, s.v. *Si contra quos.*

other litigant or an interested third party proceeded with the trial, the conferment depended on the future outcome of the trial.[12]

It should be noted here that, according to Abbas Panormitanus (1386-1453), an election for a vacant church does not *ipso facto* make the church cease to be vacant. The one elected had first to be confirmed in that election by the proper authority. Therefore, possession of the church did not obtain until the election was confirmed.[13]

In the final decretal of this title in the Constitutions, it is stated that no innovation can be made during the pending litigation. Furthermore, a cause was considered to pend once the citation had been issued by the competent judge and the party so cited had received it, or it had at least come to his notice that he had in some way been cited. The cause did not begin to pend until the party knew that he had been cited. It was sufficient for the citation to be issued by the judge in order that his judicial jurisdiction perdure.

> Quum, lite pendente nihil debeat innovari, litem quoad hoc pendere censemus, postquam a iudice compententi in ea citatio emanavit, et ad partem citatam pervenit, vel per eam factum fuit, quo minus ad eius notitiam perveniret; dum tamen in citatione praedicta talia sint expressa, per quae plene possit instrui, super quibus in iudicio convenitur.[14]

Abbas Panormitanus taught that the possessor did not cause an innovation if he made use of his possession while the trial was in process. But there would have been an innovation if he had been deprived of his possession, or if the object of controversy had been alienated, or if a privilege

[12] C. 1, *ut lite pendente nihil innovetur*, II, 5, in Clem.

[13] *Commentaria*, ad c. 1, *ut lite pendente etc.*, II, in Clem., n. 1: "Per solam electionem factam ad ecclesiam vacare, sed per confirmationem subsecutam sic. Ex quo infertur, quod si electus non confirmatus moritur in curia, eccelsia, in qua facta est electio, non vacat in curia, secus si ibi moriatur electus confirmatus."

[14] C. 2, *ut lite pendente nihil innovetur*, II, 5, in Clem.

had been petitioned for apart from all mention in the petition regarding any pending trial.[15]

In speaking of the pending of the litigation Abbas Panormitanus stated that any innovations effected after the citation had been issued were to be revoked *in pristinum statum.* There would be no bill of complaint nor a joinder of issue for the judge would act *ex officio.* However, when the deprivation of a possession took place outside of the pending litigation, the bill of complaint had to be presented and the joinder of the issue had to be instituted. The reason for this difference was that in the face of an attempt committed during the pending litigation not only was the party injured but the judge also suffered contempt through the action. If the spoliation took place outside the trial itself, then it was only the party who was affected.[16]

[15] *Commentaria,* ad c. 2, *ut lite pendente etc.,* II, 5, in Clem., n. 2: "Non scitur possessor aliquid innovare, si lite pendente utitur sua possessione, . . . sed bene fieret innovatio, si ipse possessor privaretur possessione sua, vel alienaretur res litigiosa, vel super causa impetraretur privilegium, tacita litis pendentia."

[16] *Commentaria,* ad c. 2, *ut lite pendente etc.,* II, 5, in Clem., n. 1: "Innovata lite pendente post scilicet citationem, de qua hic, revocanda sunt in pristinum statum sine libello, et contestatione litis, ex puro et mero iudicis officio: secus, ubi quis praetendit se spolitaum lite non pendente, quia tunc ad consequendam restitutionem offertur libellus, et lis contestatur, et in hoc differunt . . . et diversitatis ratio potest esse, quia in priora casu laeditur non solum pars, sed iudex contemnitur; in secundo vero tantum pars, ideo in priori casu magis iudicis officium."

CHAPTER III

PREJUDICIAL ATTEMPTS FROM THE COUNCIL OF TRENT (1545-1563) TO THE CODE OF CANON LAW (1918)

ARTICLE 1. CONCEPT OF *Attentatum*

Pellegrini († 1678) defined prejudicial attempts as all acts or their equivalents which without a reasonable cause are undertaken during the pending of the litigation or an appeal by the judge, or by a party, or by one handling the cause for them, in contempt of jurisdiction, and in prejudice of a party. It was the duty of the judge, whose honor had been violated, first of all and before everything else to revoke the prejudicial attempts.[1] In early decretal law

[1] *Praxis Vicariorum* (Venetiis, 1696), Pars III, sect. 5, n. 2. Pax Jordanus (*Elucubrationes Diversae* [3 vols., Coloniae, 1729], lib. II, tit. 16, *de attentatis*, n. 42) used the same definition for a prejudicial attmpt: "Describitur vero attentatum, seu innovatum, ut sit omnis actus, sine rationabili causa, lite, appellatione aut his aequipollentibus, pendentibus, a iudice, sive a parte, seu ab habentibus causam ab eis, in contemptum iurisdictionis, et praeiudicium partis factus, officio eius, cuius laesa maiestas, in primis, et ante omnia revocandus." Jordanus (*ibid.*, nn. 40-41) discussed the various ways in which *attentatum* and *innovatum* were sometimes used. *Attentatum* was found in the following senses: 1) "pro conatu, et nixu ad aliquem actum faciendum," 2) "quando quis, blando sermone pudicitiam alicuius impetit," 3) "pro aggravare, seu molestare," 4) "pro eo, quod praesumere," and 5) "pro eo quod fit lite pendente in contemptum iudicis, et praeiudicium partis." Then, *Innovatum*: 1) "pro renovare," 2) "pro cautionem renovare, id est, non novare, vel non extinguere," 3) "pro novum ius impetrare," 4) "pro benefiicium impetrare," 5) "pro rei statum mutare," 6) "ad novum esse reducare," and 7) "pro eo, quod fit, lite pendente, in contemptum iudicis, vel partis praeiudicium, et idem sit, quod attentare." In regard to the phrase, "sine rationabili causa," Passerini († 1677) noted: "Notandum primo circa illud verbum *sine rationabili causa attentatur*, quod illud dicitur attentari, quod fit sine rationabili causa, et sic omne irrationabiliter gestum est attentatum."—*Commentaria in Sextum Librum Decretalium* (5 vols. in 2, Venetiis, 1698), Vol. I, Lib. I, p. 495, n. 16 (hereafter cited as *Commentaria*).

the term *innovatum* was used rather than *attentatum*. This is clearly seen in the *Liber Sextus* of Boniface VIII.[2] Reiffenstuel (1642-1703) singled out this usage of the two terms after he had explained what were to be understood as *attentata*, especially when committed during a pending appeal.[3]

The question arises whether there was any difference between *litis pendentia* and *appellationis pendentia* in regard to prejudicial attempts. An answer or solution was given by Reiffenstuel. He held that there was no difference in the effect that ensued. Some difference, however, could be noted in regard to their efficient cause. The prejudicial attempts in a pending appeal referred to the attempts committed by the judge; whereas attempts in pending litigation referred to those attempts committed by one of the litigants.[4]

[2] C. 7, *de appelationibus*, II, 15, in VI°.

[3] "Attentata in proposito idem sunt ac innovata contra ius, lite, seu appellatione, pendente. Ita desumitur ex rubrica, totoque titulo, 'Ut lite pendente nihil innovetur': juncta rubrica, et 1. un. ff. 'Nihil novari appellatione interposita'; ... 'Attentata,' esse vocabulum interpretum, non iurisconsultum ... nam in iure talia appellantur, 'Innovata post appellationem'; ... non vero 'Attentata.' "—*Ius Canonicum Universum* (7 vols., Parisiis, 1864-1870), Lib. II, tit. 28, n. 249 (hereafter cited as *Ius Canonicum*).

[4] "Attentata, lite, vel appellatione pendente an differant? Conjunguntur autem simul, "Attentata lite, vel appellatione pendente.' Quia in effectu non differunt, licet possit aliqua differentia notari quoad suam causam efficientem. Nam attentata pendente appelatione, respiciunt personam iudicis, cum scilicet adeo attentata sunt: quae vero fiunt pendente lite, respiciunt personam adversarii, quia nimirum ab ipso sunt innovata."—*Op. cit.*, Lib. II, tit. 28, n. 252. Cf. Fermosinus (*Opera Omnia Canonica, Civilia et Criminalia* [2. ed., 14 vols., Coloniae, 1741], XV, p. 615, n. 4) (hereafter cited as *Opera Omnia*) stated that no prejudicial attempts are committed unless a trial is pending: "Absque lite non dantur attentata ... duo esse necessaria, ut quis dicatur attentare, scilicet pendentia litis primo, et innovatio secundo." Passerinus made the following observation in regard to attempts committed during an appeal: "Duas regulas dat decretalia ista. Prima est non solum tamquam attentata revocanda sunt ea omnia, quae post interpositam appellationem a diffinitiva in-

The general law in regard to innovations during the pending litigation is found in the various collections of papal decretals under the title, *Ut lite pendente nihil innovetur.*[5] A trial was said to pend once the citation had been issued by the competent judge, and the party so cited had received it, or he knew in some way or other that he had been cited, whether he had or had not actually received the citation. The pending of the litigation commenced, then, as soon as the party was aware that he had been cited.[6]

The most important effect of the pending of the litigation was that, during the pending litigation, no innovations were permitted. According to Maschat (1692-1747), while a cause was pending in a real action at court, the object under consideration became litigious until ownership was determined. If it was a question regarding the possession and not the ownship of the thing itself, the fact of possession became the object of controversy. In a personal action, however, it was neither the object (*res*), nor the fact of possession, but the action which became the subject matter of the litigation.[7].

De Angelis (1824-1881) treated of the general prohibition against innovations during the pending litigation if they prejudiced the plaintiff, the defendant, the object in controversy, or some right existing at the time of the

novata sunt, exceptis casibus, in quibus iura prohibent appellare, sed etiam ea omnia, quae innovata sunt intra decendium datum ad appellandum, ac si haec post interpositam appellationem innovata fuissent." —*Commentaria*, Lib. II, tit. 15, c. 7, n. 1.

[5] C. 1-5, X, *ut lite pendente nihil innovetur*, II, 16; c. 1, 2, *ut lite pendente etc.*, II, 8, in VI°; c. 1, 2, *ut lite pendente etc.*, II, 5, in Clem.

[6] C. 2, *ut lite pendente nihil innovetur*, II, 5, in Clem. Cf. also Pirhing, *Ius Canonicum in V Libros Decretalium* (ed. novissima, 4 vols., Dilingae, 1722), Lib. II, tit. 16, sect. 1, n. 1 (hereafter cited as *Ius Canonicum*); Lega, *Praelectiones de Iudiciis Ecclesiasticis* (4 vols., Romae, 1896-1901), I, n. 562 (hereafter cited as *De Iudiciis*); Wernz, *Ius Decretalium*, V, Lib. II, tit. 16, nn. 554-558.

[7] *Institutiones Canonicae* (2 vols., Romae, 1757), Lib II, tit. 16, n. 3.

trial.[8] Was there any difference, then, between *inhibitio* and *prohibitio?* Pax Jordanus taught that there was actually some difference, though he concluded that the two terms were commonly used as synonyms.[9]

Another effect of the pending of the litigation was that the object of controversy could no longer be alienated. If an alienation was undertaken, the litigious matter had to be restored, or its equivalent had to be substituted. Alienation in this sense changed the status of the object of controversy, and prejudiced the other litigant.[10]

Lega (1860-1935) briefly defined *attentatum* as anything done contrary to an *inhibitio.* He next divided inhibitions into a) inhibitions of the law (general inhibitions) and b) inhibitions of a man or a judge (special inhibitions). The general prohibition was found in the rule of law which was expressed as a precept, *ut lite pendente nihil innovetur.* This prohibition forbade any innovation or change in regard to the litigious object, as long as the trial had not been concluded by way of a definitive sentence legitimately executed, or had been temporarily delayed in some manner or or other.[11] A special prohibition was in effect as often as the judge assigned to one or both of the parties certain time limits within which judiical acts could be placed, and for-

[8] *Praelectiones Iuris Canonici* (5 vols. in 9, Romae, 1877-1891), Lib. II, tit. 16, n. 4.

[9] *Elucubrationes Diversae,* Lib. II, tit. 16, *de attentatis,* n. 2, "Inhibere, et prohibere, differunt proprie inte se: quia inhibemus coeptum, ne perficiatur; prohibemus vero, ne quid fiat... secundum tamen loquendi morem solent capi pro synonymis."

[10] Maschat, *Institutiones Canonicae,* Lib. II, tit. 16, n. 3. Cf. Devoti, *Institutionum Canonicarum Libri IV* (4. ed., 4 vols. in 3, Venetiis, 1827), Lib. II, tit. 16, § 4—(hereafter cited as *Institutiones Canonicae*). This author remarked that "si restitui nequeat, alia paris aestimationis, et pretii eius vice subrogetur, quae propterea cum naturam, et qualitates accipiat rei, quae in eius locum substituta, et supposita est, alienari non potest, nisi lis absoluta sit." Likewise, De Angelis, *Praelectiones Iuris Canonici,* Lib. II, tit. 16, nn. 6-8.

[11] *De Iudiciis,* I, n. 560. Cf. Wernz, *Ius Decretalium,* V, Lib. II, tit. 16, n. 557.

bade any prejudicial attempt to be committed during that period.[12]

By way of an example of a special prohibition, Jordanus stated that an *inhibitio* is a prohibition or precept of a superior or of the judge of appeal (*iudex ad quem*) imposed upon an inferior or upon the judge of the first instance (*iudex a quo*) not to commit an innovation, that is, a prejudicial attempt, while the appeal is being considered in the appellate court. Moreover, everyone possessing ordinary or delegated jurisdiction could impose a prohibition, provided his jurisdiction was greater than that of the person upon whom the injunction was imposed. If an inferior enjoined his superior, the precept was invalid and furnished no basis for a prejudicial attempt. Finally, the superior judge could impose a prohibition on all his inferiors, whether they were judges, parties in the cause or other persons.[13]

It must be noted that a prohibition presupposed that the judge who issued it had jurisdiction and was therefore competent to act in the cause. Consequently, in an appeal the judge of the appeal could not impose a prohibition until first he was certain that he had the jurisdiction over the appeal and that the appeal was made within the time limits established by law.[14]

In order that the judge of the appeal be able to suspend the jurisdiction of the judge of the first instance, it did not suffice that the prohibition had been made known to the parties in the cause. It was necessary also that the judge of the first instance be informed. It must, of course, be understood that the prohibition of the judge of appeal suspended the jurisdiction of the judge of the first instance only if it had been made canonically, that is, by the judge who was competent in the cause.

[12] Lega, *loc. cit.*

[13] *Elucubrationes Diversae*, Lib. II, tit. 16, *de attentatis*, n. 3. Cf. Santi, *Praelectiones Iuris Canonici* (4. ed., curante M. Leitner, 5 vols., Romae, 1903-1905), Lib. II, tit. 28, n. 46.

[14] Scaccia, *Tractatus de Appellationibus* (3. ed., Coloniae, 1717), Quaestio III, n. 30 (hereafter cited as *De Appellationibus*).

Lega held that an attempt was a species of spoliation (*spolium*). The reason was that the innovation deprived another of the peaceful quasi-possession of a right, namely, the right to retain the object of controversy in his possession until the trial was concluded. It was called a quasi-possession, since the fact of rightful possession was yet to be determined by means of the judicial process. Thus, once an attempt had been committed by the judge or by one of the litigants, the injured party had the right to an action for the declaration of the nullity of the spoliation. Such an action would be a rescissory action. Consequently, the cause could not be prosecuted further until everything had been restored to its original status.[15]

Cardinal Tuschus († 1620) in his published work *Practicae Conclusiones Iuris, in Omni Foro Frequentiores,* spoke of a cause involving prejudicial attempts as being more privileged and having more favor before the law than a cause of spoliation. The reason for this statement was that in a cause involving spoliation the injured party merely received back what had been taken; in a cause involving a prejudicial attempt, however, the injured party recovered the litigious object for the duration of the trial, retaining it in his possession, provided the sentence was in his favor, and, what was more, the honor of the judge was vindicated. Thus, the cause involving an attempt was privileged in two ways: 1) in a cause treating of spoliation the plaintiff had to prove that he was dispossessed by the despoiler, and that he was actually in possession at the time he was dispossessed. In the revocation of prejudicial attempts, however, it sufficed that the person proved that he had had possession, and that the defendant still was in possession. This held whether he proved that there was actually any act of dispossession or not. 2) In the revocation of prejudicial attempts the judge proceeded *ex officio,* that is, without the presentation of the bill of complaint and without the joinder of issue. In a cause involving spoliation, however, the plain-

[15] *De Iudiciis,* I, n. 560.

tiff had to present a bill of complaint, and there had to be a joinder of issue. By reason of these privileges, the remedy against prejudicial attempts was more favorable and more easily accomplishable than the remedies in a cause of spoliation, wherein the due process of law had to be followed.[16]

Some of the various ways in which a prejudicial attempt could be committed in pending litigation have already been indicated. One may well advert here to some of the others along with those previously mentioned. They are: 1) taking possession of the object of controversy, 2) transferring possession of the litigious object to some one else, 3) alienating the litigious object, 4) presenting a cleric to a vacant church or vacant benefice, while it continues as the object of litigation, 5) proceeding to a new election to choose a cleric to fill a vacant church, when this church was already the object of controversy and one of the litigants had died, resigned or ceded the question during the pending litigation, and 6) petitioning a rescript or privilege apart from all mention in the petition of the pending litigation.[17]

An act was not to be considered an attempt as such, if the law itself permitted the judge or a party to act, even though it would have been an attempt otherwise without the intervention of the law. A prejudicial attempt was an act contrary to a right which a person possessed. If there was no such right duly sanctioned by the law, then also there could be no question of the commission of an attempt. Tuschus (1534-1620) discussed the question whether a person committed an attempt, if he not only retained posession but also made use of the object of controversy during the pending of the litigation. His conclusion was that no prejudicial attempt would be committed in such a case.[18]

[16] Tuschus, *Practicae Conclusiones Iuris, in Omni Foro Frequentiores* (7 vols., 1 vol. Suppl., Lugduni, 1634), Vol. I, concl. 548, p. 273 (hereafter cited as *Practicae Conclusiones*). Cf. also Fermosinus, *Opera Omnia,* VIII, p. 528, n. 54.

[17] Jordanus, *Elucubrationes Diversae,* Lib. II, tit. 16, *de attentatis,* nn. 64-74.

[18] *Practicae Conclusiones,* Vol. I, concl. 542, p. 272. The following

Reiffenstuel (1642-1703) stated that the judge of the first instance did not commit an attempt when he determined the time within which an appeal was to be made. Nor did he commit an attempt in seeking to expedite an appeal.[19]

In the definition of a prejudicial attempt given at the beginning of this study, it was stated that an attempt can be committed by the following persons: a) the judge of the cause, b) a party in the litigation proceedings, or c) a person handling the cause for them, e.g., a procurator of one of the parties in the cause. In analyzing the harm done in consequence of an attempt, one sees that it is threefold: a right, in its very nature of a right, is violated; the judge is shown contempt; and one of the parties, or even both, are prejudiced.[20] When a prejudicial attempt is committed by one of the litigants, the judge is more offended than the injured party, since a prohibition pronounced by him has been held in contempt and violated.[21] If the judge commits an attempt, there is no doubt in the mind as to who the perpetrator of the prejudicial attempt really is. When one of the litigants violates the rule of law in this regard, there

authors were found to agree with Tuschus: Scaccia, *De Apellationibus*, Quaestio III, n. 70; Fermosinus, *Opera Omnia*, Vol. VIII, p. 536, nn. 8-10; Passerinus, *Commentaria*, Lib. II, tit. 15, cap. 7, n. 15; Reiffenstuel, *Ius Canonicum*, Lib. II, tit. 28, n. 251.

19 *Ius Canonicum*, Lib. II, tit. 28, n. 253: "Attentatum dici nequit, quod fit lege permittente ... quia, quod fit lege permittente, poenam non meretur ... Unde quando iudex a quo statuit appellandi terminum ad recipiendum apostolos, vel ad prosequendum appellationem, aut huiusmodi ... non censetur attentare; haud obstante, quod innovet aliquid post appellationem: quia iure permittente istud facit. Idem dicendum de aliis, quae iuvant ad faciliorem expeditionem causae appellationis: nam ista expediendo post interpositam appellationem, non censetur iudex aliquid innovare, seu attentare." This appeared to be the common opinion among the various authors, except for Barbosa (*Collectanea Doctorum* [6 vols. in 4, Romae, 1656], Lib. II, tit. 28, cap. 73, n. 28), who held: "Iudex a quo potest innovare quando tendit ad faciliorem exitum appellationis."

20 Barbosa, *op. cit.*, Lib. II, tit. 28, cap. 73, n. 30; Fermosinus, *Opera Omnia*, Vol. VIII, p. 538, n. 38.

21 Fermosinus, *op. cit.*, Vol. VIII, p. 534, n. 24.

likewise will be no doubt as to the guilty party as long as no one acts for him. Will a procurator, when acting under mandate from the party, always commit an attempt if he also violates the law which forbids innovations during the pending of the litigation or an appeal? Jordanus taught that the procurator would do so only if he had a special mandate from the party so to act, and not if he had only a general mandate for action.[22]

The possibility of the commission of an attempt by a third person other than the judge, or by one of the litigants or by the procurator was discussed by the pre-Code authors. Barbosa (1589-1649) stated that a third person does not commit an attempt and that accordingly the remedy for prejudicial attempts could not be used against him.[23] Jordanus, however, included the third party in his discussion of those who can be said to commit attempts. He naturally excluded the plaintiff, the defendant and the judge from those who he would consider as being third parties. He gave as an exmaple in this regard an Ordinary who would confer a benefice the while it continues as the object of controversy. But as to the revocation of such an attempt, Jordanus excluded it from the usual remedy for the revocation of attempts. Another means had to be employed, since, according to this author, the pending of the litigation affected the litigants and the judge, and not the others in the matter of prejudicial attempts.[24]

With reference to the perpetration of an attempt, one was always to understand that it militated against someone or something. Thus, a prejudicial attempt showed contempt

[22] *Elucubrationes Diversae*, Lib. II, tit. 16, *de attentatis*, n. 46. Cf. also Fermosinus, *op. cit.*, Vol. VIII, p. 530, n. 2.

[23] *Collectanea Doctorum*, Lib. II, tit. 28, cap. 73, n. 35.

[24] *Elucubrationes Diversae*, Lib. II, tit. 16, *de attentatis*, nn. 49-51. Cf. Fermosinus, *Opera Omnia*, Vol. VIII, p. 529, n. 8: "Tertius non dicatur attentare, nec possit contra eam remedio attentatorum uti." Passerinus, *Commentaria*, Vol. I, Lib. II, p. 257, n. 13: "Instante ergo appellante revocari ante omnia debent attentata innovata a iudice a quo vel ab altera parte. Non tamen a tertio; nam tertius non attentat."

to the judge and prejudiced the party. There was no acceptance of the act of attempt by the person injured. Dissent, then, by the person who might be injured by the attempt was an absolute requirement before there could be any question of employing the remedy against attempts, in order to repair the harm done during the pending litigation or appeal.[25]

ARTICLE 2. SENTENCES AND APPEALS

An understanding of the various kinds of sentences and of appeals is necessary in the matter at hand, since the possibility of attempts being perpetrated and of their being revoked subsequently depends upon whatever distinction actually obtains.

During the course of a trial the judge may have occasion to impose two kinds of sentences: definitive and interlocutory. A *definitive* sentence is the decision of the judge putting an end to the principal controversy. It contains either a condemnation in regard to the charges alleged in the bill of complaint or an absolution from them. An *interlocutory* sentence is one which the judge pronounces over any matter of controversy arising after the principal cause has been introduced and before the definitive sentence has been given. The interlocutory sentence is further divided into a simple interlocutory sentence (*interlocutoria simplex*) and into one having the effect of a definitive sentence (*interlocutoria vim habens definitivae*). Van Espen (1646-1728) defined the distinction between the two as follows:

> Sententia autem interlocutoria duplex est. Una habens vim definitivae, atque a sententia definitiva fere solo nomine distincta: altera mere et simpliciter interlocutoria. Prior appellatur illa senttentia, quae quidem principale negotium absolute non dirimit, sed tantum aliquem articulum causae principali incidentem aut connexum; atque eatenus interlocutoria vocatur: sed articulum talem incidentem ita dirimit, ut per hanc suam sententiam parti litiganti damnum inferat irreparabile

[25] Fermosinus, *Opera Omnia,* Vol. VIII, p. 536, n. 13.

> per definitivam, aut appellationem a definitiva; quapropter haec sententia quantumvis interlocutoria, dicitur habere vim definitivae.[26]

Schmalzgrueber († 1735) distinguished between a definitive sentence and an interlocutory sentence as follows: 1) when the word sentence is used in law without any other qualifications, it is always to be understood as a definitive sentence, unless the context or circumstances would indicate that an interlocutory sentence is to be understood. 2) A definitive sentence terminates the controversy; an interlocutory sentence does not have such an effect of finality. Furthermore, an interlocutory sentence cannot be employed in order to declare some one infamous. 3) A definitive sentence must be made absolutely, with no conditions. A citation must be issued to the defendant; the judicial order must be observed; and the sentence must be put into writing. On the other hand, an interlocutory sentence can be made conditionally; it need not be made in writing; nor is it necessary to observe the customary judicial form or to issue a citation to the defendant. 4) As a rule, an interlocutory sentence can be corrected or revoked by the same judge who imposed it, unless: a) the interlocutory sentence has already been put into execution; b) it has already been appealed and confirmed by the judge of appeal; c) it was imposed with the consent of both parties; d) it had definitive force;[27] or e) the judge of the first instance has permitted an appeal to be interposed from his interlocutory sentence, and he has been prohibited by the judge of the appeal to act any further in the cause appealed. Lastly, 5) a

[26] *Ius Ecclesiasticum Universum* (10 vols., Venetiis, 1769), Pars III, tit. 9, c. 1, nn. 6-7. An *articulus* is the assertion of the principal fact of a cause, which the plaintiff proposes to the defendant. The plaintiff must be prepared to prove his statements, if they are denied by the defendant.

[27] Pierantonelli (*Praxis Fori Ecclesiastici* [Romae, 1883], p. 152) did not agree with Schmalzgrueber on this last difference mentioned. See below at no. 2.

definitive sentence, most generally, can be appealed, whereas an interlocutory sentence cannot be.[28]

Pierantonelli, in his work *Praxis Fori Ecclesiasticum*, which was published in 1883, made four distinctions between a definitive sentence and an interlocutory sentence: 1) a definitive sentence differs from a simple interlocutory sentence, or one having the effect of a definitive sentence, in that the definitive sentence must be written and, when it is a condemnatory sentence in a criminal cause, the canonical sanction on which the penalty is based must also be set down in the written sentence. There is no requirement that the interlocutory sentence be in writing. 2) The definitive sentence cannot be revoked by the same judge after it has once been imposed; the interlocutory sentence, whether simple or one having the force of a definitive sentence, can be revoked. The interlocutory sentence can be revoked by the same judge who imposed it, provided he does so before he issues the definitive sentence. 3) The definitive sentence and the interlocutory sentence which has the force of a definitive sentence differ from a simple interlocutory sentence in that an appeal can be made from them, but not from the simple interlocutory sentence. 4) The definitive sentence and the interlocutory sentence with definitive force can be further differentiated: a) the definitive sentence can be appealed immediately by word of mouth, or after a time interval of ten days in writing; an appeal from an interlocutory sentence must be written and must include mention of the nature of the grievance upon which the appeal is made; b) an appeal from a definitive sentence has this effect, namely, that the acts of the judge of the first instance which are prejudicial to the litigants, whether after the appeal has been made, or with the time granted for making an appeal, ar considered as attempts. These attempts must, before any other judicial act is placed,

[28] Schmalzgrueber, *Ius Ecclesiasticum Universum* (5 vols. in 12, Romae, 1843-1854), Lib. II, tit. 27, n. 25 (hereafter cited as *Ius Ecclesiasticum*). Cf. also Reiffenstuel, *Ius Canonicum*, Lib. II, tit. 28, n. 264.

be revoked by the judge of the appeal, and the original status of the object of controversy be restored. But only those acts of the judge of the first instance which he places after an interlocutory sentence are considered as attempts, if they follow upon the prohibition of the judge of the second instance intimated canonically to the first judge.[29]

One must, therefore, conclude in reference to an interlocutory sentence that, although it is a judicial sentence in the true sense of the word, it does not possess the same juridic force and efficacy as a definitive sentence. Prior to the Council of Trent, an appeal was just as readily permitted from an interlocutory sentence as it was from a definitive sentence. This facility of appeal, however, was changed by the same Council (1545-1563).[30]

From the middle of the sixteenth century the freedom to appeal an interlocutory sentence was radically curtailed, unless the sentence was an interlocutory sentence with definitive force or one in which the injury to the innocent person could not be repaired by means either of a definitive sentence or of an appeal from the definitive sentence.[31] Once a person was imprisoned, for example, the harm was already accomplished and accordingly could not be repaired as if no imprisonment had ever occurred.

An appeal may be defined as the act of a person seeking redress against his superior from a higher superior or judge, for a grievance either already inflicted or about to be inflicted. Thus, it is permissible to make a judicial or extrajudicial appeal against a grievance, not only when it

[29] *Op. cit.*, p. 154: "Appellatio a definitiva effectum habet ut gesta per iudicem *a quo,* sive post interpositam appellationem, sive medio tempore inter sententiam et appellationem attentata censeantur et debeant ante omnia per iudicem appellationis revocari et in pristinum statum reduci. Ex iis vero quae per iudicem *a quo* geruntur post interlocutoriam, ea tantum attentata censentur quae subsequuntur inhibitioni per iudicem appellationis iudici *a quo* canonice factae."

[30] Sess. XXIV, *de ref.*, cap. 24.

[31] Sess. XIII, *de ref.*, cap. 1.

has been inflicted but also when a person has reason to suspect that it will be.[32]

The appeal may be of two kinds: judicial or extrajudicial. The judicial appeal is that which is interposed against judicial acts or proceedings, and can be made during three stages of the trial: 1) before the joinder of issue, 2) after the joinder of issue, but before the definitive sentence, and 3) after the definitive sentence, that is, when the appeal is made against the sentence or its execution. It is to be noted that it is after the second stage that an appeal against an interlocutory sentence is permissible. The extrajudicial appeal (*provocatio ad causam*) is that which is interposed against extrajudicial acts or decrees, by which a person considers that he has been aggrieved.[33]

An appeal is lawful and admissible only when it is interposed by a person who has the legal capacity to do so. In general, all persons can appeal judicially or extrajudicially as the case may warrant, whenever they consider themselves unjustly injured by the action of a judge or a superior. The reason for this is that an appeal is a defense granted by the positive law[34] to all persons who believe that they have been harmed or injured by the action of the judge. More particularly, the persons upon whom the grievance has been inflicted and those directly affected by it may interpose an appeal. Consequently, such persons as are unaffected by the sentence have no right to seek an appeal.

An appeal can have two effects, namely, *suspensivus* and *devolutivus*. It can begin to pend immediately upon the

[32] Schmalzgrueber, *Ius Canonicum*, Lib. II, tit. 28, n. 1: "Appellatio est ab inferiore ad superiorem iudicem provocatio facta ratione illati vel inferendi gravaminis."

[33] Lega, *De Iudiciis*, I, n. 618: "Appellatio dividitur in *iudicialem* et *extraiudicialem*, prout provocatur ad actibus iudicialibus, scilicet a sententia vel iudicis decreto; aut ab actibus extraiudicialibus, utputa a decreto Episcopi super praesentatione vel collatione beneficii."

[34] Lega (*De Iudiciis*, I, n. 619) discussed whether it is a right by reason of the natural law or of positive law.

pronouncement of a definitive sentence. While the appeal is pending, the sentence and competence of the judge are so suspended, that the sentence cannot be put into execution nor can anything be done to prejudice the right of the appellant in regard to the object of controversy. It must be understood, however, that there can be no question of the pending of a judicial appeal unless the sentence is one that can be appealed. Therefore, after the sentence of the judge has been imposed, the appeal is said to pend, since a definite time limit of ten days is established by law for the making of an appeal. If the appeal is legitimately made, it is then said to continue to pend.[35]

In regard to an extrajudicial appeal, Lega stated that its suspensive effect begins from the moment the cause is brought before the judge of the appeal. This judge will then issue a prohibition against any innovations being committed by the judge of the first instance during the pending of the appeal. After giving brief consideration to attempts committed during an appeal which has a suspensive effect, Lega added that the remedy against attempts is not a special effect of an appeal, but rather flows from the suspensive effect.[36] Bouix (1808-1870) and Wernz (1842-1914) both spoke of the remedy against attempts as being another effect of an appeal.[37]

[35] "Pendente appellatione, suspenditur vis sententiae et iudicis competentia, adeo ut hic prolatam sententiam exequi non valeat, nec aliquid innovare in re litigiosa contra ius appellantis . . . Pendentia exoritur statim ac pronunciata est sententia iudicialis definitiva, a qua potest appellari; tunc enim incipit decurrere tempus decendii statutum ad appellandum, quo decurrente, nihil est innovandum; pendentia vero prosequitur cum legitime interponitur appellatio."—Lega, *op. cit.*, I, n. 625.

[36] *Op. cit.*, I, n. 626: "At ex dictis, remedia attentatorum non esse specialem effectum appellationis, . . . sed fluere ex effectu suspensivo."

[37] Bouix, *Tractatus de Judiciis Ecclesiasticis* (2. ed., 2 vols., Parisiis, 1855), II, 288 (hereafter cited as *De Judiciis*). Wernz, *Ius Decretalium*, V, Lib. II, tit. 28, n. 697.

ARTICLE 3. PREJUDICIAL ATTEMPTS COMMITTED DURING AN APPEAL

It was previously stated that the law forbiding innovations during the pending of the litigation is equally valid for innovations during a pending appeal. Reiffenstuel held that there was no difference between the two so far as the effect was concerned; rather, it was the efficient cause that one had to look to in order to discover any difference.[38] Lega brought out this difference, perhaps a little more clearly, in regard to the efficient cause, when he stated that the pending of an appeal directly commands the judge of the first instance not to bring about any innovations in the cause appealed. Therefore, such attempts as are committed will, first of all, come about through the actions of the judge of first instance. On the contrary, in a pending litigation the prohibition against attempts is primarily directed to the litigants, forbidding them to change the status of the object of controversy in any way.[39]

The Council of Trent (1545-1563) gave but brief consideration to the question of prejudicial attempts, when it renewed the law formulated in the decretals of Boniface VIII.[40]

> Legates and Apostolic nuncios, patriarchs, primates and metropolitans, in appeals interposed before them, are bound in all causes, both in admitting appeals and in granting inhibitions after an appeal, to observe the form and tenor of the sacred constitutions, and especially that of Innocent IV, which begins, *Romana*: any custom, even immemorial, style or privilege to the contrary not withstanding: otherwise the inhibitions, the

[38] *Ius Canonicum,* Lib. II, tit. 28, n. 252.

[39] "Differentia inter attentata adversus litem pendentem et attentata in pendentem appellationem est, pendentiam appellationis directe iudicem iubere, ne aliquid innovet in casa appellationis, et hinc attentata in appellationem cum primis ponuntur a iudice.—E contra lite pendente prohibetur praecipue, ne litigantes aliquid mutent in re litigiosa."—*De Iudiciis,* I, n. 626.

[40] C. 3, *de appellationibus,* II, 15, in VI°.

procedure and all consequences thereof shall be null *ipso iure.*[41]

In a decree of the Sacred Congregation of Bishops published in 1600 and approved by Pope Clement VIII (1592-1605), a number of doubts and controversies over jurisdictional matters which involved judges of the first instance and judges of appeal were resolved. Among the various matters dealt with, it was decreed that the judge of the first instance must take care lest he commit any attempts in prejudice of the appellant, if the appeal was lawfully made. Moreover, if it should be proved by public act or by depositions of witnesses that the appellant had been unjustly treated, the judge of the appeal could enjoin, not only that the appellant should be given his lawful rights in the matter, but also that no additional attempts should be committed against him.[42]

In the eighteenth century the Congregation of the Council added the weight of its authority in the adjudication of causes involving attempts. In 1734 a cause was submitted to the Congregation which concerned attempts committed by a bishop after an appeal had been interposed by a prior general. The object of controversy in this cause was the question of making appointments to certain parish churches.

[41] Sess. XXII, *de ref.*, cap. 7: "Legati, et nuncii apostolici, patriarchae, ac primates, et metropolitani in appelltaionibus ad eos interpositis, in quibusvis causis, tam in admittendis appellationibus, quam in concedendis inhibitionibus post appellationem, servare teneantur formam, et tenorem sacrarum constitutionum, et praesertim Innocentii IV. quae incipit, Romana: quacumque consuetudine, etiam immemorabili, aut stylo, vel privilegio, in contrarium non obstantibus: aliter inhibitiones, et processus, et inde secuta quaecumque, sint ipso iure nulla."

[42] "Caveat tamen iudex a quo, ne si vere appellatum fuerit in casu appellabili, interim aliquid in praeiudicium appellantis attentet; et si per actum publicum, aut per testium depositiones constiterit, acta denegari appellanti, iudex appellationis mandato trandendi acta possit adiicere, ne interim aliquid novi contra appellantem attentetur." —Quaranta, *Summa Bullarii Earumve Summorum Pontificum Constitutionum* (Venetiis, 1622), p. 70-72.

It was asked whether atempts had been committed, and, if so, was action to be taken to repair the damage which had ensued from the attempts. The answer of the Congregation was affirmative to both of the questions.[43]

Again, in 1735, this same Congregation of the Council gave an affirmative answer to the question whether or not attempts had been committed in a cause which had been presented to it for its consideration. The attempts had been committed by an episcopal tribunal which had ordered the sequestration of the property and the money of a priest who had previously interposed an appeal to the metropolitan tribunal. The Council enjoined that the attempts were to be rigorously removed by purgation.[44]

The Sacred Congregation in 1753 once more considered a cause involving attempts. In this cause prejudicial attempts were committed by the Curia of the Church of Pescia after an appeal had been interposed to the Tribunal of the Nunciature of Florence. The prejudicial attempts consisted in proceeding in a cause without jurisdiction and in a violating of prohibitions pronounced by the Nunciature. The answer of this Congregation was that it was sufficiently established that attempts had been committed and were to be revoked according to the established procedure in a matter involving nullity.[45]

In the three sections that follow, the major decretalists and authors of the period from 1563-1918 will be studied in their teachings principally as to the attempts committed by the judge: a) during any appeal in general, b) after an appeal from a definitive or an interlocutory sentence, and c) after an interposed judicial or extrajudicial appeal.

[43] S.C.C., *Constantien.*, 24 nov. 1734—*Codicis Iuris Canonici Fontes*, cura Emi Petri Card. Gasparri editi (9 vols., Romae: Typis Polyglottis Vaticanis, 1923-1939, Vols. VII-IX ed. cura et studio Emi Iustiniani Card. Serédi), n. 3435 (hereafter cited as *Fontes*).

[44] S.C.C., *Oritana.*, 20 aug. 1735—*Fontes*, nn. 3445, 3448.

[45] S.C.C., *Piscien.*, 24 mart. 1753—*Fontes*, nn. 3627, 3632.

SECTION A. PERJUDICIAL ATTEMPTS DURING APPEALS IN GENERAL

Tuschus († 1620) in his *Practicae Conclusiones* taught that acts perpetrated after a sentence which has not yet been appealed are as equally attempts as those innovations which are committed after the appeal has been interposed.[46] According to Pirhing (1606-1679), one of the effects of an appeal was that there were to be no innovations allowed while it was pending, and, if any occurred, they were necessarily to be revoked.[47] Maranta († 1530) maintained that the appellant who attempted anything against his own appeal was to be considered as having renounced the appeal. Consequently, the judge of the first instance could proceed as though the appeal had not been made. But if the attempts were not contrary to the appeal, the judge, instead of disregarding them, had to proceed to their revocation. However, if the other party of the appeal or the judge of the first instance was guilty of the innovations, then they were to be revoked and the guilty person was to be fined the expenses.[48] If the judge unjustly anticipated the day assigned for the trial and the litigants did not consent to it, they were given the right to appeal. If any prejudicial attempts were then perpetrated after the appeal, such attempts were null and were to be revoked.[49]

Passerinus, in speaking of the time given for making an appeal, taught that the judge would be guilty of committing an attempt, if he put the sentence into execution during this period.[50] He also adverted to the situation in which an appeal was interposed after the prescribed time for the

[46] Vol. I, concl. 542, p. 272: "Facta post sententiam ante appellationem ita dicuntur attentata, sicut facta post appellationem subsequuntur in tempore." Cf. also Fermosinus, *Opera Omnia*, Vol. VIII, p. 533, n. 10.

[47] *Ius Canonicum*, Lib. II, tit. 28, sec. 8, § 5.

[48] *Speculum Aureum*, Pars VI, n. 194. Cf. also Pirhing, *ibid.*, n. 249; Fermosinus, *Opera Omnia*, Vol. VIII, p. 534, nn. 20-21; Maschat, *Institutiones Canonicae*, Lib. II, tit. 28, n. 25, Q. XVII.

[49] Pirhing, *ibid.*, n. 251.

making of appeals. If it was not known that the sentence had been given and the appeal was interposed later than the ten days, only attempts during these ten days would be forbidden. Revocation was then to take place, if any attempts were committed. On the other hand, once the ten days were over and before an appeal was interposed, if the judge executed the sentence or the other party caused any innovations, then it was not considered that any attempts had been committed. Hence, the remedy against attempts could not be used for the purpose of their revocation.[51]

De Luca (1614-1683) discussed the problem whether a cause or a sentence is appealable of its own nature in regard to prejudicial attempts. He concluded that some causes or sentences can by the very nature of the matter involved be appealed. This being so, the possible commission of attempts would have to be taken under consideration. At the time De Luca wrote, it was the general rule that all causes had this twofold effect if they were not specifically excepted by law. In those causes, however, which did not admit an appeal *in suspensivo,* no consideration was given to attempts, even though an appeal had been made, or could be made.[52]

Jordanus in speaking of the persons who could commit attempts declared that the judge of the first instance would be guilty of an attempt, if he proceeded with a cause from which an appeal had been legitimately interposed.[53] He also stated that the general rule was that, during the ten days given for an appeal, no innovations were allowable. While this time was running, the appeal could be looked upon as already made, since the two were equal so far as the effect of the attempts was involved.[54]

The acts placed by the judge of an appeal when acting

[50] *Commentaria,* Lib. II, tit. 15, c. 7, n. 16.

[51] Passerinus, *Commentaria,* Lib. II, tit. 15, c. 7, n. 26.

[52] *Theatrum Veritatis et Iustitiae* (16 vols., Coloniae Aggrippinae, 1706), *De Iudiciis,* Disc. 18, n. 28.

[53] *Elucubrationes Diversae,* Lib. II, tit. 16, *de attentatis,* n. 47.

[54] Jordanus, *op. cit.,* Lib. II, tit. 16, *de attentatis,* nn. 164-165.

invalidly were not according to Fermosinus prejudicial attempts. The reason given for this statement was that attempts committed in an invalid appeal were not to be revoked, even though the judge of the appeal had issued a prohibition, since jurisdiction did not devolve when the appeal itself was null. Thus a judge who acted during an invalid appeal also acted invalidly so far as prejudicial attempts were concerned.[55]

Devoti (1744-1820) in explaining appeals spoke of the necessity of their being legitimately interposed. He taught that, only after it was proved that the appeal was interposed within the proper time, by a person having the right to appeal, from a definitive sentence or one having definitive force, could the judge of the appeal accept the appeal and, thereby, make prohibitions against any innovations. Once it was determined that the appeal was legitimately made, the judge of the first instance could no longer act in the cause which had been appealed. Nevertheless, if he did proceed with the cause, the remedy against prejudicial attempts was available for the annulling of all innovations occurring during the appeal or within the ten days granted by law for an appeal.[56]

It was asked by Schmalzgrueber what action the judge of the first instance could take in a cause which had been appealed so as not to commit an attempt. In answering this question he cited seven different situations in which the judge of the first instance would not be guilty of such wrong doing. His general rule was that the judge of the first instance was permitted to do everything which would help the appeal and make for a more expeditious handling of the cause, or at least would not be injurious to it.[57]

[55] *Opera Omnia,* Vol. VIII, p. 524, nn. 3-4; p. 529, n. 2.

[56] *Institutiones Canonicae,* Lib. II, tit. 28, § 23.

[57] *Ius Ecclesiasticum,* Lib. II, tit. 28, nn. 115-118. Bouix (*De Judiciis,* II, pp. 288 f.) listed five actions whereby the judge of the first instance would not commit attempts.

SECTION B. PREJUDICIAL ATTEMPTS AFTER AN APPEAL FROM A DEFINITIVE OR AN INTERLOCUTORY SENTENCE

Tuschus taught that as a general rule any innovation after an appeal from a definitive sentence on the part of the judge was properly looked upon as a prejudicial attempt. But in regard to an appeal from an interlocutory sentence there was no question of attempts unless a prohibition had proceded them.[58] Passerinus maintained that the judge of the first instance could proceed with a cause in which an appeal was forbidden, though an appeal from a definitive sentence was regularly granted, unless it was expressly forbidden. He declared that the law itself sometimes permitted the judge of the first instance to put the sentence into execution, even while the appeal was pending. This action of the judge could not then be revoked as an attempt.[59] As to an appeal from an interlocutory sentence, Passerinus stated that innovations committed after such an appeal were to be revoked not immediately and before any other judicial act was undertaken, but after the appeal was reviewed and the judge was satisfied that the appeal was justly made. If the judge of the appeal, however, had issued a prohibition and decided that the cause was legitimately appealed so that it devolved to him, any innovations after the prohibition had immediately to be revoked before any further action was taken in the cause.[60]

In answering the question as to what would be an attempt after an appeal had been interposed, Bouix gave five situations in which prejudicial attempts could be committed by

[58] *Practicae Conclusiones*, Vol. I, concl. 542, p. 272. Cf. also Pellegrini, *Praxis Vicariorum*, Pars III, sec. 5, n. 40; Fermosinus, *Opera Omnia*, Vol. VIII, p. 536, nn. 1-16.

[59] *Commentaria*, Lib. II, tit. 15, c. 7, n. 3.

[60] *Op. cit.*, Lib. II, tit. 15, c. 7, n. 21. Scaccia (*De Appellationibus*, Quaestio 17, limit. 47, memb. 1, n. 28) also held that the judge of the first instance could proceed in a cause while an appeal was pending from an interlocutory sentence without committing an attempt. Consequently, there was no question of any revocation of prejudicial attempts.

the judge by reason of the pending appeal: 1) It was not an attempt, if the judge of the first instance acted beyond any prejudice to the appellant. The element of prejudice was necessary before there was any attempt. 2) When the appeal was made from a definitive sentence, whatever was done after the appeal had been interposed, or during the time between the sentence and the interposition of the appeal, became an attempt. 3) If an appeal was made from an interlocutory sentence with definitive force, then the same held for it as for the definitive sentence. 4) If there was an appeal from an interlocutory sentence not having definitive force, the appeal had no effect in regard to attempts committed after the appeal. The reason was that, after the Council of Trent (1545-1563), such an appeal was illicit and null. 5) If the appeal was made from an extrajudicial act, then whatever was done after the appeal had been interposed became an attempt.[61]

Reiffenstuel declared that, although attempts during an appeal from a definitive sentence were null *ipso iure*, it was to be understood that their nullity depended upon the injured party's desire for their annulment and petition for their revocation. Otherwise the party was said to approve them tacitly and to relinquish his right to insist on their revocation.[62]

SECTION C. PREJUDICIAL ATTEMPTS AFTER A JUDICIAL OR EXTRAJUDICIAL APPEAL

Tuschus declared that prejudicial attempts could be perpetrated after an extrajudicial appeal just as well as during the pending of the litigation or after a judicial prohibiton.[63] Passerinus concurred with this opinion, but added that the solution regarding prejudicial attempts committed after a judicial or extrajudicial appeal depended on whether

[61] Bouix, *De Judiciis*, II, 289.

[62] *Ius Canonicum*, Lib. II, tit. 28, nn. 255-256.

[63] *Practicae Conclusiones*, Vol. I, concl. 542, p. 272: "Attentata dicuntur non minus, quae facta sunt pendente lite, et post inhibitionem, quam facta post appellationem extraiudicialem."

the appeal was legitimate.[64] This, however, was an opinion not held by all the decretalists, since De Luca mentioned that there was diversity of opinions. He added that the question could only be resolved upon an appraisal of the justice or injustice of the appeal, and of the nature and the quality of the attempt.[65] In the matter of attempts committed during an appeal, Scaccia maintained that the rule to be followed was this: Whether the appeal was judicial or extrajudicial, provided it was not an appeal from a definitive sentence, attempts were never revoked before all else (*ante omnia*), unless the truth of the cause of the appeal was first verified.[66]

Article 4. Solution of the Question of Prejudicial Attempts: Their Revocation

In pre-Code law the solution of the question of prejudicial attempts was an incidental question falling within the scope of the principal question and originating from it.[67] Incidental questions could, therefore, be defined as controversies which originate from or are occasioned by the principal cause, and which are carried on between the parties alone or between the parties and third persons.[68] Incidental questions could arise at any point of development in a trial—at the beginning, during or at the end of the trial. Some of them were common to any part of the trial, such as attacking the validity of an act, contumacy, and, most especially, prejudicial attempts, since the general rule was:

[64] *Commentaria,* Lib. II, tit. 15, c. 7, n. 25.

[65] *Theatrum Veritatis et Iustitiae, De Iudiciis,* disc. 18, n. 63.

[66] *De Appellationibus, Quaestio 17,* limit, 47, memb. 1, n. 28: "(Infero) quod in materia attentatorum commissorum appellatione pendente, haec sit regula, ut sive appellatio sit iudicialis, sive extraiudicialis, dummodo appellatio non sit a sententia diffinitiva nunquam revocentur attentata ante omnia, nisi primo iustificetur veritas causae appellationis. . . ."

[67] Lega, *De Iudiciis,* I, n. 539.

[68] Lega, *op. cit.,* I, n. 536.

lite seu appellatione pendente nihil innovetur. The other incidental questions varied to the extent in which the trial had been taken cognizance of. Some were more usually found at the beginning, others in the midst of the trial, or at the end of the trial.

Generally, the procedure used in the adjudication of these incidental questions did not require the customary solemnities of a trial. The judge made use of a summary process, observing only such requirements which would terminate the cause quickly and protect the rights of those involved. The judge did not need immediately to take up the incidental question, if he deemed it more advisable to pass judgment upon it along with the definitive sentence of the principal cause. This was true for incidental questions in general, though there were exceptions. The question of prejudicial attempts furnished such an exception, though again the rule for it was not so inflexible that it could not be set aside at times.[69]

The sentence which the judge imposed in an incidental question was an interlocutory sentence.[70] Lega asked whether all incidental questions had to be resolved by means of a special sentence before the definitive sentence. Though authors did not agree on this point, Lega held with Reiffenstuel[71] that before the definitive sentence the judge had to pass sentence upon the incidental questions whose decision could not be included in or delayed to the definitive sentence.[72]

Though there was no requirement that the interlocutory sentence be put into writing, it was customary and advised to reduce it to writing. If the sentence was not put into any express form, it was necessary that the acts of the trial contain its gist or content as well as the fact of its imposition by the judge. As mentioned previously, there could be

[69] Lega, *op. cit., I,* nn. 536-544.

[70] Fermosinus, *Opera Omnia,* Vol. VIII, p. 534, n. 38.

[71] *Ius Canonicum,* Lib. II, tit. 10, n. 26.

[72] *De Iudiciis,* I, n. 541.

no appeal from this interlocutory sentence, unless it was one with definitive force. This was definitely established by the Council of Trent.[73] When deciding whether an appeal was just or unjust, this was the first factor to be considered so far as prejudicial attempts were concerned.

The judge who imposed an interlocutory sentence could revoke, correct or confirm it. The reason for this, as opposed to any such action in regard to a definitive sentence, was that an interlocutory sentence did not terminate the jurisdiction of the judge of the principal cause (*iudex ordinarius*). If the person against whom the sentence was pronounced considered that he had been treated unjustly, he could present his reasons to the judge who had imposed the sentence. The judge could then correct, revoke or confirm the sentence. When it was an interlocutory sentence with definitive force, there was room for an appeal to the higher judge.

With reference to the incidental question, therefore, cognizance was taken by the judge of the principal cause, who had to issue a citation to the adverse party and adjudicate the cause.[74] Fermosinus seemed to limit this summary process to only such attempts as were of a notorious character.[75]

SECTION A. TWO METHODS FOR REVOKING PREJUDICIAL ATTEMPTS

In the discussion of prejudicial attempts given by the various authors prior to the Code of Canon Law (1918), they were generally concerned more with the revocation of attempts than with any other consideration. In fact, it was sometimes their primary and sole consideration. The ecclesiastical lawyers defined two methods in which the

[73] Sess. XIII, *de ref.*, c. 1; sess. XXIV, *de ref.*, cc. 10, 20. These decrees of the Council corrected the law of the Decretals as found in cc. 12, 59, X, *de appellationibus*, II, 28.

[74] Lega, *De Iudiciis*, I, n. 544.

[75] *Opera Omnia*, Vol. IV, Quaestio III, n. 9. Schmalzgrueber (*Ius Ecclesiasticum*, Lib. II, tit. 28, n. 126) also supported this opinion.

revocation of attempts might be brought about. One was the ordinary way (*via ordinaria*); the other, extraordinary (*via extraordinaria*). Maranta explained this twofold way by stating very briefly: one method consisted in principally urging the office of the judge in their revocation; the second, by interposing an appeal *accessorie.*[76]

Passerinus spoke of the judge who proceeded to the revocation of prejudicial attempts when the appellant had not petitioned him to act as proceeding *summarie et ex puro officio iudicis incidenter.*[77] He added that the judge could not act summarily, when another means of restitution, other than *per viam attentati,* was required. Contempt of judge or court was a concept that was usually in the background when an attempt was under consideration by the pre-Code authors. For, as they would say, a prejudicial attempt shows more contempt to the honor of the judge who imposed a prohibition, than it does injury to one of the litigants. Passerinus mentioned such contempt as one of the causes that a judge could use as sufficient motive in proceeding *ex officio* to a revocation.[78]

In speaking of the revocation of prejudicial attempts Reiffenstuel stated that it could be accomplished in two

[76] *Speculum Aurem,* Pars VI, n. 407: "Attentata revocantur duplici via. Uno modo intentando officium iudiciis super ipsorum revocatione, secundo modo, accessorie, prosequendo appellationem." Barbosa (*Collectanea Doctorum,* Lib. II, tit. 28, c. 73, n. 40) asserted: "Attentata revocari possunt quandoque ordinario remedio quandoque extraordinario iudicis officio." Cf. Pellegrini, *Parxis Vicariorum,* Pars III, sec. 5, nn. 12, 14 and 15. Passerinus (*Commentaria,* Lib. II, tit. 15, c. 7, n. 7) restricted the extraordinary method: "Hoc tamen remedium revocationis attentatorum per viam attentatorum est extraordinarium, et propterea ei non est locus, quando poest agi via ordinaria." Jordanus, *Elucubrationes Diversae,* Lib. II, tit. 16, *de attentatis,* nn. 170-171; Fermosinus, *Opera Omnia,* Vol. VIII, p. 533, n. 13; Schmalzgrueber, *Ius Ecclesiasticum,* Lib. II, tit. 28, n. 129; Reiffenstuel, *Ius Canonicum,* Lib. II, tit. 28, n. 257; Bouix, *De Judiciis,* II, 289.

[77] *Commentaria,* Lib. II, tit. 15, c. 7, n. 5.

[78] *Op. cit.,* n. 29: "Inhibitione quaque praemissa innovata contra inhibitionem revocantur etiam ex solo officio Iudicis . . . cum innovatio contineat manifestam iudicis offensam."

ways—the *via ordinaria* and the *via extraordinaria.* A party was to proceed by the *via ordinaria,* when a direct petition for the revocation of the prejudicial attempt was made along with the principal cause. If this method was used, the attempts were revoked, not immediately, but at the end of the trial. If the *via extraordinaria* was used, the party requested the judge to act *ex officio* in revoking the prejudicial attempts. This was said to be done, then, *per remedium attentati,* that is, the judicial order was not observed. When this method was employed, there was a suspensive effect, so that the principal cause was set aside until the prejudicial attempts committed after a definitive sentence had been revoked *ante omnia.*[79]

SECTION B. DEFINITE TIME GRANTED FOR PETITIONING A REVOCATION

Justice, in order to be properly and rightly administered, requires that court proceedings should not be protracted beyond a reasonable time. It would even appear that it demands swift measures in resetting the balance that has been disturbed. Nothing is more reprehensible than finding court proceedings which have been unduly protracted to the frustration, particularly, of the injured party. Granted that this is so, it will also be conceded readily that the administration of justice could not properly be furthered by the hasty preparation of proofs and defenses by the parties, or by the hurried formulation of the sentence by the judge. Equity, therefore, demands that sufficient time be given to all matters concerned.

Hence, in the trials or appeals in which prejudicial attempts occurred, the party that considered itself aggrieved was granted the period from the beginning of the litigation or appeal (*litis pendentia*) to the conclusion of the cause to petition for a revocation.[80]

[79] *Ius Canonicum,* Lib. II, tit. 28, nn. 257-259.

[80] Maranta, *Speculum Aurem,* Pars VI, n. 402. Pellegrini (*Praxis Vicariorum,* Pars III, sec. 5, n. 26) added that this was true whether

Passerinus declared that, although the appellant did not petition the revocation of the prejudicial attempts before the trial should proceed any further, he could request it at any time before the conclusion of the cause. His reason was that a party did not renounce what the law itself did not insist upon when the joinder of issue took place. He included the petition for a revocation of prejudicial attempts in this category.[81]

The conclusion of the cause designated the end of the time granted by the judge to the parties for presenting their proofs to the court. Once all the proofs were presented and the judge was satisfied that the cause was properly constructed, a decree was issued which brought about the close of the probatory part of the litigation (*terminus probatorius*).[82]

SECTION C. PROCESS FOLLOWED IN REVOCATION

A cause in a trial can be drawn up in two ways: 1) as an ordinary process, or 2) as a summary process. In both there is necessarily the plaintiff and the defendant. Upon presenting satisfactory proof to the court, the plaintiff will be granted his request of the court; if it is not satisfactory,

an appeal was made from a definitive sentence, from an interlocutory sentence, or from extrajudicial acts. Cf. also Scaccia, *De Appellationibus*, Quaestio III, n. 81; Fermosinus, *Opera Omnia*, Vol. VIII, p. 527, nn. 45-46; Maschat, *Institutiones Canonicae*, Lib. II, tit. 28, n. 25, Q. XVIII; Schmalzgrueber, *Ius Ecclesiasticum*, Lib. II, tit. 28, n. 129.

[81] *Commentaria*, Lib. II, tit. 15, c. 7, n. 14: "Imo licet appellans non petierit revocationem attentatorum ante omnia, eam potest petere in quacumque parte litis, dum tamen id fiat ante conclusum in causa. Etenim per litis contestationem non renuntiat quis aut recedit ab illis, quae ordinem iuris non requirunt, inter quae est petitio revocationis attentatorum."

[82] Lega, *De Iudiciis*, I, n. 529.

[83] *De Iudciis*, I, n. 591: "Notio substantialis processus summarii ... haec est ut, praetermissa subtili observatione solemnis ordinis iudiciarii, simpliciter et de plano sine strepitu et figura iudicii procedatur, et quodammodo sola facti veritate ... ad citius expediendam causam pronuntietur."

the defendant is acquitted. In the summary process the solemnities of the ordinary process are not required. The ordinary process must have a bill of complaint, a summons and a joinder of issue. The summary process omits the presentation of the bill of complaint, since it suffices for the plaintiff to present his petition orally; and abstracts also from the joinder of issue. Furthermore, in the summary process the solemn conclusion of the cause is unnecessary. Consequently, the difference between the two is to be found more in the judicial form than in the matter involved in the cause. In both the plaintiff must prove the allegations relating to the charges made or events preferred by him. Lega gave a very concise notion as to what the summary process is, namely, a proceeding without the subtle observations of the solemn judiciary order, simple and lacking the usual atmosphere of a court trial, wherein the object of inquiry is solely the truth of the fact previously considered. The purpose, then, is that the question will be settled expeditiously.[83]

In the summary process the following must always be included: 1) the citation of the party, 2) the oath to speak the truth, 3) the opportunity for the parties to present the circumstances of fact (*positiones*) and the assertions which are to be refuted by the other party (*articuli*), 4) the interrogation of the litigants by the judge, and 5) the admittance of necessary proofs and legitimate defenses.[84]

The question of prejudicial attempts, was therefore, to be treated as an incidental question adjudicated by way of a summary process.[85]

Before the judge instituted the proceedings for revocation, he had first to decide whether the attempts were preceded by a prohibition and the making of the appeal was justified.[86] It could happen that the appellant did not inform the judge of the first instance or the other litigant that he had made an appeal. If this was so, then the judge

[84] Lega, *op. cit., I*, nn. 591-597.

[85] See page 35.

and the other party did indeed commit attempts because of the fact that an appeal had been interposed, but nevertheless they were not guilty of the so-called *vitium attentati,* nor was there to be any revocation of the attempts.[87] Pellegrini maintained that it was not necessary to inform the judge and the other litigant of an appeal, if it was an extrajudicial appeal that was interposed.[88]

Pellegrini gave the following as the mode of procedure: the appellant was to appear before the judge of the appeal (*iudex ad quem*) with the request that the prejudicial attempts be revoked *ante omnia.* The judge was then to act upon the plaintiff's petition, unless he was satisfied that it could be included with the imposition of the definitive sentence at the conclusion of the principal cause.[89] It was stated by Jordanus that the procedure was to be conducted without the usual judiciary order and summarily; neither a bill of complaint nor the joinder of issue was required; the judicial terms (*termini*) were not observed. This was to be the mode of procedure when the judge acted *ex officio.* But as often as the revocation was to be effected at the petition of the party, a summons and a judicial examination of the cause (*causae cognitio*) were necessary.[90] Bouix maintained that the appellant was free to request that the revocation be enacted either before the principal cause was concluded or along with it.[91]

Accordingly as the appeal was judicial or extrajudicial, the revocation of the attempts varied. In judicial appeals, Maranta declared that all prejudicial attempts were to be revoked even those which were not directly contrary to the

[86] Pellegrini, *Praxis Vicariorum,* Pars III, sec. 5, n. 40; Fermosinus, *Opera Omnia,* Vol. VIII, p. 536, nn. 1-6.

[87] Maranta, *Speculum Aureum,* Pars VI, n. 402.

[88] *Praxis Vicariorum,* Pars III, sec. 5, n. 23; also Maschat, *Institutiones Canonicae,* Lib. II, tit. 28, n. 25, Q. XVIII.

[89] *Op. cit.,* Pars III, sec. 5, n. 27.

[90] *Elucubrationes Diversae,* Lib. II, tit. 16, de attentatis, nn. 188-192.

[91] *De Judiciis,* II, p. 289.

appeal; in extrajudicial appeals, only those which were contrary to the appeal.[92]

In discussing this difference between the two kinds of appeal and the revocation of attempts, Fermosinus explained the requirement that in a judicial appeal all prejudicial attempts, even though not directly contrary to the appeal, had to be revoked. In an extrajudicial appeal, however, only those directly contrary to the appeal. His reason was that a judicial appeal directly suspended the jurisdiction of the judge of first instance. In an extrajudicial appeal the jurisdiction of a judge acting extrajudicially was not suspended. Therefore, only those attempts that were directly contrary to the appeal were to be revoked.[93]

1. Revocation "Ante Omnia"

The authors and commentators were in general agreement that prejudicial attempts were to be revoked before all else (*ante omnia*), if they were committed after a definitive sentence or one with definitive force.[94] Pirhing, in ex-

[92] *Speculum Aureum,* Pars VI, n. 401: "In appellatione iudiciali, revocantur omnia attentata, etiam quae non sunt directo contra appellationem, sed in extrajudiciali revocantur solum ea, quae sunt contra appellationem, et non alia." Pirhing (*Ius Canonicum,* Lib. II, tit. 28, sec. 8, nn. 245, 252) agreed that the *remedium attentati* could be used in both appeals. He restricted its use, however, in extrajudicial appeals, for he required that the appeal be legitimately interposed; likewise attempts perpetrated after the appeal were not to be revoked, unless they were contrary to it. Cf. also Pellegrini, *Praxis Vicariorum,* Pars III, sec. 5, n. 24. Altimarus (*Tractatus de Nullitatibus,* Rub. IX, quaes. 45, n. 8) disagreed to the extent that no prejudicial attempts committed during an extrajudicial appeal were to be revoked.

[93] "Appellatio iudicialis, etiam in uno articulo, sive habeat connexitatem cum totam causa, sive non in totum, et quoad totam causam suspendit iurisdictionem iudicis. Sed quia appellatio extraiudicialibus non suspendit iurisdictionem, ex quo extraiudicialiter proceditur; ideo effici ut revocetur, dumtaxat quod est in gravamen appellationis, seu contra appellationem."—*Opera Omnia,* Vol. VIII, p. 524, nn. 10-11. Cf. Schmalzgrueber, *Ius Ecclesiasticum,* Lib. II, tit. 28, n. 125.

[94] Tuschus, *Practicae Conclusiones,* Vol. I, concl. 543, p. 272; Pirh-

plaining the revocation *ante omnia* of prejudicial attempts committed after an appeal from a simple interlocutory sentence, declared that it first had to be proved that the judge of second instance had prohibited the judge of first instance from acting further in the cause.[95]

As to when the revocation was not to be *ante omnia,* Tuschus maintained that, if an appeal had been made before the definitive sentence and the judge of first instance had proceeded with the cause, then the revocation was to come after the *conclusio in causa.*[96] Pirhing declared that prejudicial attempts were not to be revoked *ante omnia,* even though the appeal was pending, in those instances which did not legally permit an appeal after the sentence. The reason for this was that, since such an appeal was made neither *in suspensivo* nor *in devolutio,* there was no justification for revoking the attempts *ante omnia.* Moreover, even in an appeal from a definitive sentence, there could be no revocation before it was proved that the sentence had been pronounced, that an appeal had been interposed, and that an attempt had been committed.[97] Passerinus indicated five situations in which the revocation of prejudicial attempts *ante omnia* was precluded. They were 1) legitimate custom, 2) confusion as to the prejudicial attempts, 3) ensuing grave scandal or some other moral impossibility, 4) the lessening of divine worship, and 5) the necessity of a definitive sentence to rescind them.[98]

If the prejudicial attempts were committed during an

ing, *Ius Canonicum,* Lib. II, tit. 28, sec. 8, nn. 241, 244; Passerinus, *Commentaria,* Lib. II, tit. 15, c. 7, n. 1; Scaccia, *De Appellationibus,* Quaestio III, n. 47; Fermosinus, *Opera Omnia,* Vol. VIII, p. 535, n. 42; Schmalzgrueber, *Ius Ecclesiasticum,* Lib. II, tit. 28, n. 119; Reiffenstuel, *Ius Canonicum,* Lib. II, tit. 28, n. 261.

[95] *Op. cit.,* Lib. II, tit. 28, sec. 8, n. 244; Passerinus, *op. cit.,* Lib. II, tit. 15, c. 7, n. 27; Fermosinus, *op. cit.,* Vol. VIII, p. 534, n. 32.

[96] *Op. cit.,* Vol. I, concl. 547, p. 273.

[97] *Ius Canonicum,* Lib. II, tit. 28, sec. 8, n. 242.

[98] *Commentaria,* Lib. II, tit. 15, c. 7, n. 11.

extrajudicial appeal, Scaccia[99] and Fermosinus[100] both declared that the appeal had first to be proved as just. Mashcat held that the appeal from an interlocutory sentence also had to be proved as just before the revocation could be effected, unless a prohibition of the judge of the appeal preceded the attempts.[101]

2. Proof Required from the Petitioner of the Revocation

After the injured party had submitted his petition to the court and the judge had cited the other party, the petitioner had to prove three things before the prejudicial attempts, committed while an appeal was pending, could be revoked in an appellate tribunal *ante omnia*: 1) that a definitive sentence or one having definitive force had been pronounced, 2) that an appeal from the sentence had been interposed, and 3) that an attempt had been committed.[102] Schmalzgrueber, in speaking of the needed justification of or warrant for the appeal before the prejudicial attempts could be revoked, stated that the judge of the appeal could deal with the question of their revocation even before the appeal was proved to be just, that is, with the question whether the reason for the appeal was just and legitimate. This procedure could be used in an appeal from an alleged definitive sentence or from one having definitive force.[103]

[99] *De Appellationibus*, Quaestio 17, limit. 47, memb. 1, n. 28.

[100] *Opera Omnia*, Vol. VIII, p. 525, n. 17.

[101] *Institutiones Canonicae*, Lib. II, tit. 28, n. 25, Q. XVIII. Cf. also Reiffenstuel, *Ius Canonicum*, Lib. II, tit. 28, n. 263.

[102] Pellegrini, *Praxis Vicariorum*, Pars III, sec. 5, n. 17; Scaccia, *De Appellationibus*, Quaestio 12, n. 41; Jordanus, *Elucubrationes Diversae*, Lib. II, tit. 16, *de attentatis*, n. 191; Fermosinus, *Opera Omnia*, Vol. VIII, p. 527, n. 41; Schmalzgrueber, *Ius Ecclesiasticum*, Lib. II, tit. 28, n. 119; Reiffenstuel, *Ius Canonicum*, Lib. II, tit. 28, n. 260.

[103] *Ius Ecclesiasticum*, Lib. II, tit. 28, n. 119: "Quaeritur... quid requiratur, ut revocari possint, et debeant attentata post appellationem? Resp. Hic distinguendum est inter sententiam definitivam, et interlocutoriam: *si appellatum sit a sententia definitiva, vel inter-*

Article 5. Tribunal for Revocation

The tribunal competent for revoking the prejudicial attempts was determined by the general rule found in the definition of an attempt:

> Attentatum, seu innovatum, est omnis actus, sine rationabili causa lite, appellatione, aut his aequipollentibus, a iudice, seu a parte, aut ab habentibus causam ab eis, in contemptum iurisdictionis, et praeiudicium partis factus, *officio eius, cuius fuit laesa maiestas in primis, et ante omnia revocandus.*[104]

Accordingly it was the duty of the judge who had been contemned by the perjudicial attempt of one of the litigants to proceed to its revocation.[105] Tuschus declared that the attempts had to be revoked by the judge of the appeal when the innovations proved prejudicial to the appeal.[106] This same opinion was held by Pirhing, who gave the following as his reason: the judge who takes cognizance of the principal cause shall also adjudicate the questions connected with it, that is, the incidental or accessory causes. Therefore, the revocation of attempts as accessory to a cause of appeal, depending on whether the appeal had been legitimately interposed, came within the competence of the judge of the appeal.[107]

locutoria vim definitivae habente, sufficit, si fuerit appellatum legitime; unde in petens attentata revocari tria haec probaverit, sc. esse definitive pronunctiatum, esse appellatum, et postea attentatum, vel innovatum aliquid, audiri debet a *iudice ad quem,* et ante omnia revocari, quae interim acta sunt: neque necesse est appellationem esse iustificatam, vel ut constet, aut probetur causam appellandi veram, et legitimam esse."

[104] Italics inserted by the writer. Cf. page 14.

[105] Barbosa, *Collectanea Doctorum,* Lib. II, tit. 28, c. 73, n. 41; Pellegrini, *Praxis Vicariorum,* Pars III, sec. 5, nn. 2, 28; Passerinus, *Commentaria,* Lib. II, tit. 15, c. 7, n. 32; Jordanus, *Elucubrationes Diversae,* Lib. II, tit. 16, *de attentatis,* n. 42.

[106] *Practicae Conclusiones,* Vol. I, concl. 544, p. 273.

[107] *Ius Canonicum,* Lib. II, tit. 28, sec. 8, n. 255. Cf. Pellegrini, *op. cit.,* Pars III, sec. 5, nn. 23-24; Fermosinus, *Opera Omnia,* Vol. VIII, p. 533, n. 16; Schmalzgrueber, *Ius Ecclesiasticum,* Lib. II, tit. 28, n. 129; Reiffenstuel, *Ius Canonicum,* Lib. II, tit. 28, n. 265.

The exception to this general rule was the following: when the attempts had been committed after a definitive sentence or a sentence having definitive force, the judge of first instance could revoke them in order to facilitate the outcome of the cause.[108] Passerinus maintained that the same still held true, even though the judge of second instance had prohibited the judge of first instance from any further action in the cause, since the prohibition had reference to whatever militated against the appeal.[109]

The purgation of prejudicial attempts was effected in two ways: 1) through the sentence of the judge,[110] and

[108] Passerinus, *op. cit.*, Lib. II, tit. 15, Quaest. 1, art. 16, n. 430; Fermosinus, *Opera Omenia,* Vol. VIII, p. 533, n. 16.

[109] *Op. cit.*, Lib. II, tit. 15, Quaes. 1, art. 16, n. 432.

[110] The following example of a formula for such a sentence is taken from the *Elucubrationes Diversae* (Lib. XIV, tit. 14, *formula sententiae in causa attentatorum,* n. 230), of Jordanus: "Christi nomine invocato, pro tribunali sedentibus et solum Deum prae oculis habentibus per hanc nostram diffintivam sententiam, quam de iuris peritorum consitio, etc., in his scriptis ferimus, et vertuntur instantia, inter N.N. actricem ex una, et quemdam N.N. reum conventum de, et super spolio, et purgatione attentatorum, rebusque aliis in actis causae, et causarum huiusmodi latius deductis, et illorum occasione partibus ex altera, iudices specialiter deputati, dicimus, sententiamus, et declaramus voto Reverendiss. D. Cardinalis Sancti Clementis, possessionem, seu occupationem castri cum sui iuribus, et pertinentem per eundem N.N. post inhibitiones, de quibus in actis legitime executa, apprehensam, et captam, fuisse, et esse attentatam, et innovatam; illamque cum omnibus inde secutis, quatenus de facto processerunt, revocanda fore, et esse, et revocamus, ipsumque N.N. a detentione, et occupatione huiusmodi in totum tollendum, et amovendum fore, et esse, et amovemus, et tollimus, et praefatam N.N. pristinum suum statum, et possessionem, in quibus ante huiusmodi attentata, et inhibitiones fuerat, plenarie, restituendam, et redintegrandam, fore, et esse, restituimus, ac redintegramus; mandatumque desuper opportunum de illam restituendo, et amovendo respective decernendum, et relaxandum fore, et esse, ac decernimus, et relaxamus, iuxta formam commissionum desuper praesentatarum, molestationesque, vexationes, pertubationes, et impedimenta quaecumque per praefatum N.N. eidem D. N.N. super praemissis quomodolibet praestitas, factas, et illatas, factaque, praestita, et illata, fuisse, et esse temerarias, iniquas, indebitas, et iniustas, temerariaque, iniqua, indebita, et iniusta, ac de

2) through compliance with the imposed sentence on the part of the person who committed the attempt. Jordanus referred to the latter with the expression *cessio partis*. The sentence of the judge was not only to be pronounced but also to be put into execution. In the sentence itself, the requirements with reference to the restoration of the object of controversy, and regarding the expenses, fruits and damages were to be duly indicated.[111]

The party, first of all, showed compliance with the sentence by renouncing the prejudicial attempt. This had to be done unconditionally.[112] Secondly, he had to restore the fruits and pay the expenses.[113] Finally, when the restoration of the object of controversy was enjoined, he had to return the object of controversy or make a proper substitution for it.[114]

facto praesumpta, illasque, et illa eidem N.N. praefatae dominae N.N. facere minime licuisse, neque licere de iure, et propterea in, et super illis eidem N.N. perpetuum silentium imponendum fore, et esse, ac imponimus: et nihilominus eundem N.N. in fructibus a tempore occupationis citra, praemissorum occasione perceptis, ac in expensis in huiusmodi causa legitime factis, condemnandum fore, et esse, et condemnamus: quorum, et quarum liquidationem, et taxationem respective nobis imposterum reservamus. Et ita cum voto praedicto dicimus, omni meliori modo, etc.

Ita pronunciavi cum voto Illustriss. Card. S. Clementis."

[111] Jordanus, *op. cit.* Lib. II, tit. 16, *de attentatis*, n. 203; Pellegrini, *Praxis Vicariorum*, Pars III, sec. 5, n. 28; Fermosinus, *Opera Omnia*, Vol. V, p. 519, Quaes. 7, nn. 9-10, 34, 36.

[112] Jordanus, *ibid.*, n. 205; Pellegrini, *loc. cit.*

[113] Maranta, *Speculum Aureum*, Pars VI, n. 406; Pirhing, *Commentaria*, Lib. II, tit. 28, sec. 8, n. 253; Pellegrini, *loc. cit.;* Jordanus, *loc. cit.;* Fermosinus, *op. cit.*, Vol. VIII, p. 538, nn. 34, 36; Pierantonelli, *Praxis Fori Ecclesiastici*, p. 154.

[114] Jordanus, *loc. cit.*

PART II
CANONICAL COMMENTARY

CHAPTER IV

THE DEFINITION AND NOTION OF A PREJUDICIAL ATTEMPT AS GIVEN IN THE CODE OF CANON LAW

In the consideration of incidental questions[1] in the Code of Canon Law,[2] the treatment of *attentata*[3] or prejudicial attempts is taken up after that of contumacy[4] and the intervention of a third party.[5] The definition of a prejudicial attempt is found in canon 1854:

> *Attentatum est quidquid, lite pendente, aut altera pars adversus alteram aut ipse iudex adversus alterutram vel utramque partem innovat, parte dissentiente et in eius praeiudicium; sive innovatio respiciat litis mtaeriam, salvo tamen praescripto can. 1672, 1673, sive respiciat terminos partibus a iure vel a iudice assignatos ad ponendos certos actus iudiciales.*

Within this determination of the matter to be discussed in the canonical commentary, three important, even basic, elements for an *attentatum* or an attempt are found. They are: a) the active subject, i.e., one of the litigants or the judge, and the passive subject, i.e., one or both of the parties;[6] b) the object, i.e., the matter of the trial or the

[1] Canons 1837-1857

[2] *Codex Iuris Canonici, Pii X Pontificis Maximi iussu digestus, Benedicti Papae XV auctoritate promulgatus, Praefatione, Fontium Annotatione et Indice Analytico-Alphabetico, ab Emo Petri Card. Gasparri Auctus*, Romae: Typis Polyglottis Vaticanis, 1917; Reimpressio, 1949.

[3] Canons 1854-1857.

[4] Canons 1842-1851.

[5] Canons 1852-1853.

[6] Goyeneche, *De Procesibus Breves Adontationes ad L. IV. Codicis Iuris Canonici* (1 vol., 2 parts, Romae, 1947), Pt. 2, p. 130 (hereafter cited as *De Processibus*).

judicial terms, and c) the effect, i.e., an innovation in prejudice of a dissenting party or parties.[7]

These elements may also be termed conditions for an attempt, and so it is found in the commentaries of various authors. At first this difference in enumerating the elements or conditions for a prejudicial attempt is somewhat confusing, since it would appear, at first glance, that what one of the authors decides upon as the necessary conditions for a prejudicial attempt are not necessarily those demanded by another. Is it less confusing to have three elements, which can be looked upon as being the basic ones, within which the other conditions are actually combined, or would it, perhaps, be more precise to have each condition set out separately, inasmuch as it is possible? The latter of these two possibilities seems more acceptable for being less likely to offer confusion. Accordingly it will be the method here to be followed.

However, lest the method here chosen appear too arbitrary, one should first by referring to the various authors ascertain what elements or conditions they stressed. Of the authors consulted, three made no explicit mention of conditions, as such.[8]

The following authors set down four conditions: Roberti,[9]

[7] S.R.R., *Decisiones*, XX (1928), dec. XVI, p. 160, n. 7.

[8] Lega-Bartoccetti, *Commentarius in Iudicia Ecclesiastica iuxta Codicem Iuris Canonici* (3 vols., Romae, 1938-1941), III, 893 ff. (hereafter cited as *Commentarius*); Noval, *Commentarium Codicis Iuris Canonici*, Lib. IV, *De Processibus*, Pars I, *De Iudiciis* (Augustae Taurinorum: Marietti, 1920), pp. 398 ff. (hereafter cited as *De Iudiciis*); Ferreres, *Institutiones Canonicae* (2. ed., 2 vols., Barcinone: Eugenius Subirana, 1920), II, 337.

[9] *De Processibus* (2 vols., Romae, 1926; Vol. I, 4. ed., Romae, 1956), II, n. 430: "A) Actus ponatur quod praeiudicium afferat alterutri vel utrique parti, sive quod rem litigiosam in discrimen adducat aut iuris assecutionem difficiliorem efficiat, sive quod violet terminos processuales... b) Actus peragatur a iudice vel ab alterutra parte... c) Actus ponatur sine consensu partis vel partium quibus potest praeiudicium afferre... d) Actus ponatur 'lite pendente.'..."

Cappello,[10] and Regatillo.[11] They are: 1) The act must be placed during the pending of the appeal; 2) either one of the parties or the judge must have been the subject of the act; 3) It must be prejudicial to the party or parties who give no consent or dissent; 4) It must have reference to the litigious matter or the judicial terms.

Among those setting down three conditions, there are Wernz-Vidal and Vermeersch-Creusen:[12] 1) A change in the litigious matter or judicial terms, 2) prejudice to the party or parties, and 3) without the consent of the party or parties.

[10] *Summa Iuris Canonici* (3 vols., Vol. III, 3. ed., Romae, 1948), III, 298: "Quatuor requiruntur ex canone 1854: 1° Ut innovatio respiciat aut litis materiam (exclusa rei sequestratione) aut terminos ad ponendos certos actus iudiciales partibus a iure aut a iudice statutos... 2° Ut innovatio fiat cum praeiudicio partis vel partium; 3° Ut fiat cum dissensu partis vel partium; 4°Ut fiat lite pendente."

[11] *Institutiones Iuris Canonici* (2 vols., Santander, Sal Terrae, 1942), II, 241: "A) Actus ponatur a parte vel a iudice. b) In praeiudicium alterius partis vel utriusque... c) Dissensus partis vel partium. d) Actus ponatur, lite pendente...." Cf. Blat, *Commentarium Textus Codicis Iuris Canonici*, Lib. IV, *De Processibus* (Romae, 1927), p. 361 (hereafter cited as *De Processibus*); Cocchi, *Commentarium in Codicem Iuris Canonici* (8 vols., Vol. VII, 4. ed., Taurinorum Augustae: Marietti, 1946), VII, 333 (hereafter cited as *Commentarium*); Marchesi, *Summula Iuris Canonici* (4 vols., Vol. III, *De Processibus*, Albae Pompeiae: Editiones Paulinae, 1953), III, 179.

[12] Wernz-Vidal, *Ius Canonicum* (7 vols., Vol. VI, Romae, 1927), VI, nn. 572, 574: "Ergo attentatum committitur per mutationem circa possessionem rei vel quasi possessionem iuris, vel per concessionem actionis, si haec fiant parte dissentiente et in eius praeiudicium." Vermeersch-Creusen, *Epitome Iuris Canonici* (3 vols., 6 ed., Mechliniae-Romae, 1937-1946), III, 105: "Attentatum tribus elementis constat, sc. mutatione iuris de quo est controversia vel iuris ad agendum concessi; praeiudicium partis adversae; dissensu huius partis." Cf. Augustine, *A Commentary on the New Code of Canon Law* (8 vols., Vol. VII, *Ecclesiastical Trials*, St. Louis, Mo.: B. Herder Book Co., 1921), VII, 298 f. (hereafter cited as *A Commentary*); Giménez Fernandez, *Instituciones Juridicas en la Iglesia Catolica* (2 vols., Saeta, 1942), II, 262 f. (hereafter cited as *Instituciones Juridicas*); Goyeneche, *De Processibus*, I, pt. 2, p. 131.

Coronata goes beyond these groups above-mentioned by demanding that six conditions be met before there is any prejudicial attempt. For its existence there is postulated: 1) An innovation in regard to the litigious matter or the terms assigned by the law or by the judge to the parties; 2) an innovation contrary to a prohibition of the law or of the judge; 3) an innovation perpetrated while the trial is pending; 4) an innovation prejudicial to the party or the parties; 5) an innovation undertaken regardless of the dissent of the party or parties, and 6) an innovation executed by the judge or by one of the parties.[13]

Since such a diversified view is found among the authors, some confusion does ensue. The wording of canon 1854, especially the word *"quidquid"* in relation to the rest of the canon, must therefore be given very close attention if one is to determine precisely what is necessary before the other canons on prejudicial attempts become operative. Consequently, before all else, it will be necessary to determine the conditions regarding which the judge needs to demand full verification before he will accept a suit or institute one *ex officio* for the declaration of the nullity of a prejudicial attempt.

In order to keep the subject matter as definite as possible, the following conditions are to looked to as essential, so much so that, though only one be unfulfilled, there will be no attempt which can be given judicial cognizance as falling within the canons of the Code on prejudicial attempts:

1. The innovation must be placed during the time that the trial or appeal is pending.

[13] *Institutiones Iuris Canonici* (5 vols., Vol. III, 4. ed., Taurini-Romae, 1956), III, n. 1385 (hereafter cited as *Institutiones*): "Ut attentatum habetur requiritur: a) innovatio circa materiam litis aut circa terminos a iure aut a iudice partibus assignatos; b) innovatio contra inhibitionem iuris aut iudicis; c) innovatio quae fiat lite pendente; d) innovatio in praeiudicium partum vel partis; e) innovatio facta parte vel partibus dissentientibus; f) innovatio facta a iudice aut ab altera parte."

2. The cause of the innovation must be one of the parties or the judge.
3. There must be an innovation or a true change of the judicial situation in regard to the litigious matter or the judicial terms.
4. The innovation must have been undertaken contrary to the will of one or both of the parties.
5. The innovation must be prejudicial to one or both of the parties.

ARTICLE 1. THE INNOVATION DURING THE PENDING OF THE TRIAL

The concept of inhibition or prohibition[14] is very closely connected with that of the pending of the litigation, so far as an attempt is concerned.[15] Though the term "prohibition" is not expressly used in the canons governing prejudicial attempts, it is to be understood as contained there in by reason of canon 1725, 5°, in relation to the pending of the litigation.[16]

For a better understanding, this prohibition may be defined as a declaration or injunction forbidding some action. Thus, in pre-Code law there was the title, *Ut lite pendente nihil innovetur.*[17] In the Code of Canon Law there are two kinds of prohibitions: the one emanates *a iure* and the other derives *ab homine.* [18] A prohibition emanating *a iure* is one which the law itself establishes. Therefore it can also be called a general prohibition (*inhibitio iuris seu generalis*). If it derives *ad homine,* then the judge determines it. A prohibition determined by the judge (*inhibitio specialis*) and not by the law obtains the same force as a prohibition

[14] Cf. *supra,* page 17.

[15] Wernz-Vidal, *Ius Canonicum,* VI, nn. 569, 570: "*Attentare* in sensu iuridico huius vocis et in materia iudiciali est aliquid contra *inhibitionem* facere."

[16] "Lis pendere incipit; et ideo statim locum habet principium '*lite pendente, nihil innovetur.*' " (Cf. canon 1889, § 1.

[17] Cc. 1-5, X, *ut lite pendente etc.,* II, 16. Cf. *supra,* page 8.

[18] Cf. *supra,* page 17.

of law. This is so, since, whether it is a general or a special prohibition, the right is granted to the party or the parties of a trial that what is so defined shall not be transgressed.[19]

Within the general prohibition as found in the Code, there can be seen a twofold division. In canon 1725, 5°, the prohibition is so general that it forbids prejudicial attempts both during the pending of the trial and the pending of the appeal noted in canon 1889, § 1.[20] However, in this latter canon there is specifically determined what shall not take place, that is, what particular innovation is forbidden: namely, putting into execution a sentence from which an appeal has been made with a suspensive effect.[21]

In regard to the special prohibition, it will arise as often as the judge assigns to one or both of the parties terms for the placing of judicial acts either at the introduction of the cause, during its construction, at its definition, or at the execution of the sentence.[22]

Thus, there is manifest the most basic element of a prejudicial attempt: the fact that the law itself or the judge in his legal right has established a prohibition, whose violation effects a change or innovation. Without such a prohibition and subsequent innovation or attempt[23] there is

[19] Wernz-Vidal, *Ius Canonicum,* VI, n. 570; S.R.R., *Decisiones,* X (1918), *Dec.* XI, n. 12.

[20] Cf. *supra,* page 15.

[21] Wernz-Vidal, *op. cit.,* VI, n. 570: "Altera qua speciatim prohibetur, ne executioni mandetur sententia a qua appellatum est cum *effectu suspensivo* et habetur can. 1889, talis enim appellatio litis pendentiam producit seu continuat." Cf. Ferreres, *Institutiones Canonicae,* II, p. 337, n. 776.

[22] Lega-Bartoccetti, *Commentarius,* II, 894: "Aliae habentur *inhibitiones ab homine* quotiescumque iudex sive in introductione, sive in instructione, sive in definitione et executione, assignat . . . terminos. . . ." Wernz-Vidal, *op. cit.,* VI, n. 570: "Inhibitio *specialis* hominis seu a iudice inducitur per concessionem dilationum seu temporis ad actus iudiciales preficiendos in triplici iudicii periodo (*instructionis, definitionis, executionis*)."

[23] Cf. *supra,* page 15, at note 3.

no attempt which can be taken cognizance of as coming under the canons governing this incidental question.[24]

In regard to the prohibitions which a judge may impose there arises the question whether or not a party will commit an attempt or cause an innovation, if he has not been informed about the prohibition. Here the question turns simply on the party's ignorance of a special prohibition. In canon 1725, 5°, the prohibition of the law states that no innovation is to be undertaken during the pending of the litigation. Whatever controversy was carried on before the Code on whether or not attempts were rescissible or *ipso iure* null has been settled by canon 1855, § 1. This canon clearly contains an invalidating clause.[25] Therefore, since canon 16, § 1, states that no ignorance of invalidating laws excuses, unless that be expressly so stated in the law, ignorance of canons 1725, 5°, and 1855, § 1, will not render an act placed in violation of these canons anything less than an attempt which is null *ipso iure*.

It is questionable whether this conclusion is true also of the violation of a special prohibition committed in ignorance. Can it be argued that an attempt will exist as null *ipso iure*, if no knowledge of the special prohibition is had at the time the act, which would otherwise be an attempt, is undertaken? It is the opinion of the writer that, unless a

[24] Wernz-Vidal, *Ius Canonicum*, VI, n. 570: "*Attentare* in sensu iuridico huius vocis et in materia iudiciali est aliquid contra *inhibitionem* facere." Lega-Bartoccetti, *Commentarius*, II, 894: "Si quid innovetur contra *inhibitionem*, committitur *attentatum*." Noval, *De Iudiciis*, p. 398: "Ne litigans, qui rem litigiosam timet amittere sententia iudiciali, illam in deteriorem statum redigeret, inhibitae fuerunt iam veteri iure tum cuilibet parti, tum ipsi iudici quaecumque *innovationes* in re litigiosa in praeiudicium alterius partis. Illae innovationes vocatae sunt attentata. . . ." Cappello, *Summa Iuris Canonici*, III, n. 298; Cocchi, *Commentarium*, VII, n. 206; Roberti, *De Processibus*, II, n. 429.

[25] Roelker, *Invalidating Laws* (Paterson, New Jersey: St. Anthony Guild Press, 1955), p. 141. Reiffenstuel (*Ius Canonicum*, Lib. II, tit. 16, nn. 20, 21) held that they were null *ipso iure*, whereas Lega (*De Iudiciis*, I, n. 583) maintained that they were rescissible.

party has previous knowledge of a special prohibition, he will commit no attempt. The reason is that a prohibition of a judge is, in fact, a particular law binding two litigants. Until this law is properly promulgated, that is, made known to the interested parties, it cannot be said to bind one who is ignorant of it. This latter statement is more evident, if one briefly considers the pending of the litigation as brought about by the citation of the defendant. Before a trial can be said to pend, the citation must be legitimately communicated to the defendant (can. 1725). Among the requirements that are necessary before it can be said that the defendant has been cited, canon 1712, § 2,[26] states that an official intimation of the citation must be given to the defendant. Hence he must know that he has been cited. Without knowledge of the citation, there is no pending of the litigation; likewise, without knowledge of the prohibition, there can be no commission of a prejudicial attempt.

SECTION A. THE PENDING TRIAL

It is now necessary to determine exactly the time when a trial or an appeal is said to begin to pend, and, also, when this time is at an end. This determination is necessary because, though there is conceivably the possibility of a prejudicial attempt being committed outside of a pending trial or appeal, such an attempt will not fall within the prescription of the canons on attempts. The condition which would be lacking in such a case is the requirement that the litigation be pending.[27]

According to canon 1725, once the citation as noted in canon 1711, § 1,[28] is legitimately made, or once the parties have appeared in court of their own accord, the trial is said

[26] "Denuntiatur autem reo, et, si sint plures, singulis."

[27] Canon 1725, 5°: "lite pendente"; can. 1854: "lite pendente"; can. 1889, § 1, "lite pendente."

[28] "Libello vel oralis petitione admissa, locus est vocationi in ius seu citationi alterius partis."

to begin to pend.[29] Immediately upon the pending of the litigation, the prohibition of law, "no innovation shall be made during the pending of the litigation," is in force.

It must now be determined what is required to satisfy the principle of canon 1725. Upon this determination the pending of the litigation takes place. It is to be concluded, therefore, that no prejudicial attempts which are null *ipso iure* can be committed prior to this time in procedural law.

That a citation is necessary can be proved from the natural law itself. When a plaintiff presents his bill of complaint to the court, he has one purpose in mind, namely, that the court should decide in his favor and oblige the defendant to render satisfaction according to the tenor of his petition. But to condemn a person to yield to the demands of another without a hearing and an opportunity to present a defence in his own behalf is contrary to reason itself. If a person who knows that he is being named as a defendant presents himself to the court for the purpose of litigating the case before the citation is actually issued, then it would be superfluous to issue a citation. If the demands of the natural law are thus adequately fulfilled without the issuance and intimation of the citation, then the Code of Canon Law makes no further demands. This fact is clearly stated in canon 1711, § 2.[30]

Furthermore, the citation is so necessary, except in the instance just discussed, that without it the sentencing of an absent person and the whole judicial proceedings are *ipso iure* null and void.[31] Any act which would otherwise constitute an attempt during the time of the pending of the litigation would not be an attempt, even though all the other procedural acts seemed valid. The pending of the

[29] "5°. Lis pendere incipit; et ideo statim locum habet principium: '*lite pendente, nihil innovetur.*' "

[30] "Quod si partes litigantes sponte coram iudice se sistant ad causam agendam, opus non est citatione, sed actuarius significet in actis partes sponte sua iudicio adfuisse."

[31] Wernz-Vidal, *Ius Canonium,* VI, n. 383. Vidal argued from canons 1723, 1894. Cf. also *ibid.*, n. 393, at note 48.

trial must have taken place. Without this pending no consideration can be given to a suit for the declaration of the nullity and the revocation of the prejudicial attempt.

In the canons governing citations,[32] there are indicated three methods by which the citation can be intimated or made known to the defendant. The first method is the ordinary way according to the Code.[33] Here the *cursor* (summons-server) gives the decree of citation to the defendant. At the time this transaction takes place the *cursor* must, in the presence of the defendant, sign his own name on the citation with a notation of the day and hour when this took place.[34] At that juridic moment (the handing over of the citation to the defendant) the citation is considered as legitimately made. The defendant is obliged to accept the citation, saving any objections he might have to the trial until he appears in court.[35]

Canon 1717, § 3, provides for the possibility that the defendant cannot be found at his place of residence when the *cursor* comes to deliver the summons. In this case the intimation of the citation can be effected by the court messenger's leaving the citation with a member of the family or one of the household employees,[36] provided they are willing to accept it and promise to deliver the citation to the defendant as soon as possible. If these conditions are not verified, then the cuort messenger is to return the citation to the judge.[37]

The second method, namely, registered mail with a request for a return receipt, may be advisable when too great a distance of some other reason makes it difficult for the

[32] Canons 1711-1725. Cf. also canons 1842-1851.

[33] Canon 1712, § 2: "Denuntiatur autem reo, et, si sint plures, singulis." Canon 1717, § 1: "Citationis scheda, si fieri poterit, per Curiae cursorem tradenda est ipsi convento ubicumque is invenitur."

[34] Canon 1721.

[35] Wernz-Vidal, *Ius Canonicum,* VI, n. 389.

[36] Wernz-Vidal, *loc. cit.,* "... intimationem *ad domum* facere potest."

[37] Canon 1717, § 3.

court messenger to give the citation to the defendant in the ordinary way.[38] Canon 1719 states that, if another reliable way in consequence of the law or in the light of local conditions is available, then it also may be used.

The extraordinary mode of citation is called by canon 1720 the edictal citation (*citatio per edictum*). It is extraordinary because it may be used only after the methods indicated in canons 1717 and 1719 fail. The reason for their failure is given in the first paragraph of canon 1720, namely, whenever the place of the defendant's residence is still unknown after diligent inquiry.[39] The edictal citation, containing all the elements of the ordinary citation,[40] is to be affixed to the doors of the Curia for a period of time designated by the judge. It is also to be inserted in some public newspaper, such as the diocesan paper. If both of these means cannot be used, then either of them will suffice.[41]

According to the authors,[42] citations may be classified as personal or edictal. A personal citation is immediately made known to the defendant either directly by some public person, (*cursor*, court messenger, summons-server)[43] or indirectly by way of registered mail,[44] or by members of the household of the defendant.[45] If the citation is published either as a public announcement (posted on the doors of the Curia) or as a notice in the newspaper, it is called an edictal citation, as was already seen.[46]

A doubt arises as to when in point of time the edictal citation can be said to be legitimately made. This is so, since

[38] Canon 1719.

[39] "Quoties, diligenti inquisitione peracta, adhuc ignoratur ubi commoretur reus, locus est citationi per edictum."

[40] Canons 1715, 1723.

[41] Canon 1720, § 2. The latter seems to be preferable in the United States.

[42] Wernz-Vidal, *Ius Canonicum*, VI, n. 380; Lega-Bartoccetti, *Commentarius*, II, 526; Coronata, *Institutiones*, III, n. 1239.

[43] Canon 1717, § 1.

[44] Canon 1719.

[45] Canon 1717, § 3.

[46] Canon 1720.

the requirements for the ordinary citation are expressly set forth in the canons.[47] In regard to the edictal citation, however, one must combine elements from other canons with those set down in canon 1720.

It must, first of all, be noted that the place of residence cannot be said to be unknown, unless a diligent but futile search has previously been made.[48] An edictal citation has the same force as a personal citation for three reasons: 1) the judge directs that it is to be issued in place of the personal citation;[49] 2) it must include everything demanded of a personal citation according to canons 1715, 1723, and 3) it must be intimated to the defendant also.[50] When the place of residence is unknown to the judge and it is important either to the common good or to some private individual to have the matter settled juridically, an edict having the force of a citation is issued. This edict, just like the personal citation, can come to the notice of the defendant.[51] The edictal citation, since a citation must be intimated to the defendant,[52] needs to be intimated also. Therefore the edict is to be understood as intimated—in full accord with the demand contained in canon 1725—when it is proclaimed to all by being posted on the doors of the Curia and published in a newspaper (diocesan or secular). However, it will not be considered as properly intimated until the time within which it is to appear, as determined by the judge, has run out.[53]

[47] Canons 1715, 1723.

[48] Canon 1720, § 1.

[49] Canons 1717, 1720.

[50] Canons 1717, 1719, 1720.

[51] Lega-Bartoccetti, *Commentarius*, II, p. 534, n. 8: "Edictum editur vim habens citationis quod verosimiliter non potest ad aures non pertingere rei conventi. . . ."

[52] Canon 1712, § 2.

[53] Lega-Bartoccetti, *loc. cit.*: "At cum citatio *denunciatione* eget uti explicatum est, exinde edictum denunciari intelligitur per eiusdem *editionem* in publicum eo meliori modo, quo magis edictum in publicum vulgetur seu omnibus fidelibus in notitiam deveniat. Ad hoc statuit canon: 1) edictum affigendum esse ad fores Curiae, per tempus prudenti iudicis arbitrio determinandum."

Wernz-Vidal take under consideration the possibility that a cause could be regarded as pending though a personal citation had not been issued, and though the defendant had not appeared in court of his own accord. Such an instance could be verified if it were altogether superfluous or impossible for a citation to be intimated to the defendant through the ordinary means provided by the common law. Thus, if a crime had such notoriety that it could not possibly be concealed, or if the perpetrator deliberately concealed himself or made it impossible for the citation to reach him, then a personal citation would not need to be issued. But an edictal citation would be in order.[54]

In order to know that one can say that a citation has legitimately been made, one must verify the presence of the elements that are essential to a citation.[55]

Under pain of nullity[56] the citation must contain: a) the name of the judge; b) a judicial precept to appear in court; c) the name of the person or persons being cited. This should include all that is necessary to make positive identification, such as place of domicile, profession, title (*procurator, curator, etc.*); d) mention of the time when and the

[54] *Ius Canonicum,* VI, n. 384: "Citatio vero non debet fieri, si est superflua aut plane impossibilis, veluti si crimen est ita notorium, ut nulla tergiversatione possit celari, v.g. si reus in flagranti deprehendatur, aut si reus dolose latitet aut aliud praestet impedimentum, ne citari possit. Nam finis citationis est, ut reus sciat, actionem sibi intentam esse, iam vero reus illa affectata ignorantia et occultatione satis probat, se scire citationem suam esse decretam. Neque citatio requiritur, si citandus esset reus in loco, ad quem non tutus patet aditus apparitori, vel si periculum esset in mora. Quae in praxi intelligenda sunt de personali intimatione; semper autem praestet ut non omittatur citatio per edictum (Arg. can. 1729)."

[55] Lega-Bartoccetti, *Commentarius,* II, 537: "Citatio est initium iudicii et... habet duo momenta, nempe ipsum decretum quo iudex admisso actoris libello mandat super hoc conveniri reum ut respondeat; en *decretum citationis,* seu primum momentum; dein hoc decretum debet parti denunciari, en *secundum momentum;* et ex hisce duobus momentis seu elementis, aeque substantialibus, coalescit citationis actus."

[56] Canons 1715, 1723.

place where the defendant is to appear; e) the name of the plaintiff (first and last names); f) the signature of the judge and the notary as well as the seal of the tribunal, and g) a statement of the purpose of the plaintiff's petition, at least in general terms, and of his reasons for presenting the petition to the tribunal. If a sufficient expression of the plaintiff's contention is lacking, then the citation is invalid according to canons 1715 and 1723. Notice regarding the latter need not be furnished if a copy of the bill of complaint itself is transmitted along with the citation.[57]

If the decree of citation has been drawn up and issued, but has not yet been intimated to the defendant, the object or matter of the petition as contained in the bill of complaint does not become litigious, nor does the cause become properly the judge's before whom the action was instituted.[58]

The second element which is essential for the emergence of the pending of the litigation is the actual intimation of the citation to the defendant.[59] More particularly, the intimation of the citation is the act whereby the decree of citation is made known to the person being cited. The ordinary means, as determined by the Code, for bringing this notice

[57] Wernz-Vidal, *Ius Canonicum*, VI, n. 387.

[58] Canon 1725, 1°; 1568. Cf. Noval, *De Iudiciis*, n. 408. Cf. also lega-Bartoccetti, *Commentarius*, II, p. 528, n. 8, where it is stated that the decree of citation according to canon 1725 has these effects, though the degree itself had not been duly intimated: (1) "*res non sit amplius integra,*" (2) "*causa fiat propria iudicis coram quo actio instituta est.*" This conclusion is not valid, since can. 1725 demands that the citation must have been legitimately intimated first before the five effects of that canon will actually follow. Coronata (*Institutiones*, III, n. 1249) holds that 2°, 3° and 4° of canon 1725 become effective, even though the citation has not been intimated. In this statement he contradicts himself, for simultaneously (p. 179, n. 1249, note 6) he stated: "*Quae igitur non est legitime peracta, nullum effectum iuridicum producit.*"

[59] C. 1, *ut lite pendente nihil innovetur,* II, 5, in Clem. Cf. page 12-13 *supra*. S.R.R., *Decisiones,* X (1918), dec. XI, n. 12: "Litis pendentia quoad effectus iuridicos non inducitur per oblationem libelli; sed requiritur ut citatio sit emissa, et ad partem citatem pervenit." See also Wernz-Vidal, *Ius Canonicum*, VI, n. 571.

to the defendant is the use of a court messenger (*cursor*)[60] or summons-server. The court messenger is that member of the tribunal who is designated to inform others of judicial acts. This being so, canon 1717 in §§ 1 and 3 stipulates that the decree of citation, if possible, is to be served on the defendant (*pars conventa*) wherever he is found. If the court messenger is unable to find the defendant, he may then leave the decree with a member of the family or the household, provided such a person is prepared to assure him that the decree of citation will be presented to the defendant as soon as possible. If the citation cannot be accordingly communicated, the court messenger must then return the decree to the judge who issued it. The judge must, after receiving the decree, act in accordance with canons 1719 and 1720. It is to be noted here that the pending of the litigation does not begin once the decree has been given to a member of the family or the household. It is still required that the defendant actually receive the citation or, at least, know of its existence. Until this is so, there cannot be present any committing of prejudicial attempts which *ipso iure* are null and void in their effect.[61]

It could happen that the defendant may refuse to accept the citation or, if he does accept it, will tear up without having read it. If such action takes place, canon 1718 states that a defendant who refuses to accept the decree of citation is to be regarded as having been legitimately cited.[62] Wernz-Vidal state that the moment the citation is in the possession of the person being cited the citation is legitimately made, even though the defendant does not read it.[63]

Once it has been established, in reference to the personal citation, that the citation has been drawn up by a competent

[60] Canons 1591, 1717, 1719-1722.

[61] Canon 1717, § 3.

[62] "Reus qui citatoriam schedam recipere recuset, legitime citatus habeatur." Cf. Reg. 66, R.J., in VI°; Lega-Bartoccetti, *Commentarius*, II, 533.

[63] *Ius Canonicum*, IV, n. 389. Cf. also Coronata, *Institutiones*, III, n. 1245.

judge, issued by him and finally intimated to the defendant, and that the decree of citation contains all that is required by canons 1715 and 1723 to make it valid, the citation can then be regarded as legitimately made. This is also true in regard to the edictal citation.

It is evident that the citation by way of edict is to be resorted to only after the judge has decided that the personal citation is impossible. Since it is an extraordinary means, it is to be used only in exceptional instances. The reason for this is that it can easily be without effect and occasion the loss of much time. Thus, when the citation by way of edict is to be used, every means at hand is to be employed for gaining the effect which the law contemplates.

The duration of time for which the edict is to be affixed to the doors of the Curia and the notice of it is to appear in the newspaper is left to the discretion of the judge. Since there should be no waste of time, the judge should try to designate a length of time which, in so far as he can foresee, will accomplish the purpose of the edictal citation as soon as possible. Once this period of time has expired, the litigation will begin to pend.[64]

The rule of law, namely, *ut lite pendente nihil innovetur,* is equally applicable during a pending appeal. The appeal begins to pend immediately upon the definitive sentence, according to canons 1854 and 1881. The difference between prejudicial attempts committed either during the proceeding of a trial or during a pending appeal can be explained as follows. Once an appeal begins to pend,[65] the judge may usually not put into execution the sentence which he has pronounced. The litigious matter in this instance remains completely protected by the principle *"lite pendente nihil innovetur"* (can. 1854 and 1881). Hence prejudicial attempts during a pending appeal are committed principally by the judge. On the other hand, during the pending of the litigation in the first instance the prohibition against in-

[64] Cf. *supra*, p. 63 f.

[65] Cf. canons 1854, 1881-1882, 1889.

novations relates principally to the litigants themselves, forbidding them to bring about any change in the litigious matter.[66]

In regard to appeals,[67] canon 1889 states that an appeal with suspensive force causes the execution of the sentence to be suspended and the full force of the principle applies that "pending the litigation no innovation shall be made."[68]

An appeal *in devolutivo tantum* does not suspend the execution of the sentence, though the litigation is still pending in reference to the merits of the cause.[69] The judge can, therefore, put the sentence into execution without committing a prejudicial attempt. However, every appeal is *in suspensivo,* unless the law explicitly states otherwise. If, then an appeal *in suspensivo* has been interposed and the judge who pronounced the sentence proceeds to put the sentence into execution, he commits a prejudicial attempt.[70] There are two instances given in the Code in which the judge may order a provisional execution of the sentence notwithstanding the pending appeal *in suspensivo.*[71]

[66] Reiffenstuel, *Ius Canonicum,* Lib. II, tit, 28, n. 252. Cf. *supra,* p. 15. Also Lega-Bartoccetti, *Commentarius,* II, 1005.

[67] Cf. canons 1881-1884, 1889 and 1902.

[68] To translate the word *lis* in *lite pendente* or *litis pendentia* as "trial" tends to lead to some confusion. In the minds of many persons the connotation of trial is restricted to the juridicial processes carried on in the court of first instance, whereas they reserve "appeal" for the trial or lawsuit carried on in the court of second instance. Therefore, to avoid such confusion and the needless repetition of "pending trial or appeal," the writer proposes for the future to translate the Latin word "*lis*" as litigation or lawsuit.

[69] Caon 1889, § 1. Appellatio in suspensivo executionem appellatae sententiae suspendit ac propterea in suo robore permanet principium: '*lite pendente nihil innovetur*'; appellatio autem in devolutivo tantum, non suspendit executionem sententiae, licet lis adhuc pendeat circa meritum causae.

§ 2. Omnis appellatio est in suspensivo, nisi aliud in iure expresse caveatur, firmo praescripto can. 1917, § 2.

[70] Cf. canons 1889, 1881, 1854.

[71] Canon 1917, § 2. Iudex tamen potest sententiae, quae nondum transiit in rem iudicatam, provisoriam executionem iubere:

Of the two kinds of appeal (*in suspensivo* and *in devolutivo*), it is chiefly the appeal made *in suspensivo* that is of concern here. An appeal begins to pend once there has been pronounced a definitive sentence from which an appeal can be interposed.[72] Upon the pronouncement of a definitive sentence, the appeal must be interposed before the judge who pronounced the sentence (*iudex a quo*), within ten days from the notification that the sentence has been pronounced.[73] As these days begin to run, the appeal itself begins to pend. This pending of the appeal continues, at most, for ten days, or also less if an appeal is actually interposed.[74] Moreover, with the beginning of the prosecution of the appeal[75] the pending of the appeal continues and the principle of law, "no innovation shall be made," is in force.[76]

The pending of the litigation is, therefore, to be understood as the situation comprising that period of time which runs from the beginning to the end of the judicial process. To be more exact, it extends from the intimation of the citation to the defendant (can. 1725) to the sentence which

1°. Si agatur de provisionibus seu praestationibus ad necessarium sustentationem ordinatis.

2°. Si alia gravis urgeat necessitas, ita tamen ut, concessa provisoria executione, per cautiones, fideiiussiones aut pignora satis consultum sit indemnitati alterius partis casu quo executio revocanda sit.

[72] Cf. canons 1854, 1881, 1880, 1889. Roberti, *De Processibus,* II, n. 476.

[73] Canon 1881.

[74] Cf. canons 1881, 1902, 1889. The ten days' duration is to be computed as a *tempus utile.* Note canons 1885 and 1733.

[75] Canon 1883. The month granted for the prosecution of the appeal is likewise computable as a *tempus utile.* Cf. Michiels, *Norma Generales Iuris Canonici* (2 vols., 2. ed., Parisiis-Tornaci-Romae: Desclée et Socii, 1949), II, 275.

[76] Canon 1889. Lega-Bartoccetti, *Commentarius,* II, 1005: "Haec pendentia appellationis constituitur statim ac pronunciata est sententia iudicialis *definitiva* a qua potest appellari; tunc enim incipit decurrere tempus *decendii* statutum ad appellandum, quo decurrente, *nihil est innovandum;* pendentia vero prosequitur usque dum legitime absolvitur iudicium appellationis."

defines the matter under controversy, thus causing it to become a matter irrevocably adjudged.[77] Apart from the definitive sentence which has become irrevocably adjudged, there are other means by which the pending of the litigation is terminated.[78] These will be taken up in more detail in the following section.

Until the joinder of issue[79] takes place, however, the pending of the litigation may be regarded as the time during which the trail remains still in a state of prospectiveness. In this state of prospectiveness all the effects of a legitimately intimated citation obtain.[80]

The concept of the pending litigation is basic to a trial. It has its inception according to the provision of canon 1725, 5°.[81] As the trial progresses from its preliminary stages, so also evolves the concept of the pending of the litigation, which begins as a part of the introductory phase. Each factor in the growth of this concept carries it on toward its ordinary, proper conclusion—a definitive sentence, from which no further appeal is given.[82] The litigation is also ended by means of a compromise,[83] a decisive oath,[84] and other means established by the Code.[85] The pending of the litigation commences within the "Introduction of the Cause" and is accurately determined by the joinder of issue. The joinder of issue can be defined as the formal con-

[77] Canon 1902. Res iudicata habetur:

1°. Duplici sententia conformi;

2°. Sententia intra utile tempus non appellata, aut quae, licet appellata coram iudice *a quo*, deserta fuit coram iudice *ad quem*.

3°. Sententia definitiva unica, a qua non datur appellatio ad normam can. 1880.

[78] Cf. canons 1849, 1925, 1834, 1929.

[79] Canons 1726-1731.

[80] Canons 1725, nn. 1°-5°.

[81] Cf. *supra*, pp. 60 ff.

[82] Canon 1880.

[83] Canon 1925.

[84] Canon 1834.

[85] Cf. canons 1849 and 1929.

tradiction of the plaintiff's petition by the defendant with a view to litigating the issue in court.[86]

The purpose of the joinder of issue, according to canon 1726, is to determine the object or matter of the trial. Inasmuch as the determination of the object of the trial is effected by the joinder of issue, the joinder of issue is itself a part of procedural law, having a basis in the natural law, since the trial naturally postulates that the object (contested by the parties and to be adjudicated by the judge) must be accurately determined. With reference to the possible commission of a prejudicial attempt, the trial can be said to begin, in the broad sense, with the citation or the defendant's voluntary appearance according to canon 1725. In the strict sense, however, the litigation is said to begin with the joinder of issue, since the object of litigation is only then defined by the parties.[87]

Wernz-Vidal state that the joinder of issue is the foundation of the whole canonical process, so much so that in all causes not excepted in the Code the complete canonical process and any sentence pronounced are null and void, if the joinder of issue has been omitted.[88]

Can a prejudicial attempt, then, be committed, if the litigation has simply begun to pend in that the joinder of issue has not taken place, but nevertheless there is present an

[86] Canon 1726.

[87] Lega-Bartoccetti, *Commentarius*, II, 583: "At instantiam assumere debemus non stricte et formaliter quae incipit tantum lite contestata (c. 1732) sed magis large seu quatenus *virtualiter* et *effective* initium habet a momento quo decretum citationis per denunciationem remissum est adversae parti adeo ut habeatur *litis pendentia* (c. 1725, n. 5) et in eodem largiori sensu quo in c. 1740, § 1, statuitur posse instantiae renuntiari in *quolibet statu* et *gradu iudicii* seu etiam ante litem contestatam sed postquam iudicium coeptum est per denunciationem decreti citationis." Cf. also *ibid.*, 589; Coronata, *Institutiones*, III, nn. 1259, 1262.

[88] *Ius Canonicum,* VI, n. 399: "Litis contestatio cum sit fundamentum universi processus canonici, in omnibus causis a iure ecclesiastico non exceptis adeo necessaria est, ut illa omissa totus ordinarius processus canonicus ipsaque sententia lata sint nulla et irrita."

act that fulfills all the necessary conditions specified for prejudicial attempts?[89]

The answer to this question is to be found among the various ways in which the instance of a litigation (*litis instantia*), considered in its broader meaning as beginning according to canon 1725, can be ended. More particularly, the peremption of the instance is the basis upon which the solution of the problem will depend. The pending of the litigation runs parallel with the instance of the litigation once the joinder of issue has taken place. The joinder of issue and the instance of the litigation, considered in the strict sense of canon 1732, take place simultaneously.[90] The exact moment (*terminus a quo*), however, from which we are to consider the instance of the litigation as beginning is a matter of considerable importance here. It would be a defect in the law if the pending of the litigation took place and then could cease shortly after because no joinder of issue had ensued. Though in the Code there is not specified any time limit within which the joinder of issue must take place, nevertheless the canons on the abatement of a lawsuit (*peremptio instantiae*) do designate the time that it is terminated (*terminus ad quem*).[91]

The concept of the abatement of the lawsuit is to be found in canon 1736. It is the following: unless there is an impediment, if no procedural act is placed in the tribunal of first instance for two years, or in an appeal for one year, the instance (lawsuit) is abated. If an appeal is under consideration, the sentence in question becomes irrevocably adjudged.[92] The canons that govern abatement or peremption are included under the same title of the Code, Title VIII, which treats of the instance of the litigation. This

[89] Canon 1854.

[90] Canon 1732. "Instantiae initium fit litis contestatione...."

[91] Canons 1736-1739.

[92] "Si nullus actus processualis, quin aliquod obstet impedimentum, ponatur in tribunali primae instantiae per biennium aut in grado appellationis per annum, instantia perimitur, et in altero casu sententia per appellationem oppugnata transit in rem iudicatam."

specific allocation of the canons on peremption could seem to restrict their operation to the instance of the litigation in its strict sense.[93] This restriction, however, does not seem to obtain. It is necessary to have recourse to the broader concept of the instance of the litigation, namely, as beginning according to the provision of canon 1725. Otherwise it could happen that a cause might be begun upon the citation's legitimate intimation, but would be held "in a state of prospectiveness" for an indefinite period of time beyond the two years fixed in first instance and one year in appeals, if the joinder of issue did not take place. Such an indefinite period of waiting would seem entirely foreign to the whole tenor of the Code, especially since certain causes are to be explored for a judgment as expeditiously as possible.[94] Thus in computing the starting point of peremption it will be necessary to use the distinction of Lega-Bartoccetti.[95] If difficulties are to be avoided in regard to the computation of the beginning and termination of the peremption and the attempts within the period of peremption, then the term of peremption must be looked upon, in the broad sense, as beginning with the pending of the litigation. If the joinder of issue is omitted, a prejudicial attempt cannot be committed after two years have elapsed from the beginning of the pending litigation in a trial's first instance or after one year in a trial's second instance, provided no judicial act has been placed in these respective periods of time.

SECTION B. THE TERMINATION OF THE *Litis Pendentia*

The pending of the litigation has been traced, thus far,

[93] Lega-Bartoccetti, *Commentarius*, II, 583, 589; Coronata, *Institutiones*, III, nn. 1259, 1262.

[94] Canon 1620, "quamprimum"; canons 1616; 1709, § 3; 1856, § 2, "breviter."

[95] *Commentarius*, II, 583, 589. Coronata, *op. cit.*, III, n. 1262: "Instantia de qua hoc in c. 1736 intelligitur in lato sensu, quae incipit non litis contestatione sed a momento quo decretum citationis denuntiatur reo convento, quo momento initium habet litis pendentia ad normam c. 1725, n. 5."

through its inception[96] to the instance of the litigation, which originates with the joinder of issue.[97] The pending of the litigation and the instance of the litigation then continue together, that is, run parallel to each other. This parallelism of the two, however, lies precisely therein that they do not at any time coalesce. This fact is demonstrable by way of comparison of the canons.[98] As long as the instance is not terminated, the pending of the litigation will continue at the same time, and this state (their parallelism) will not cease until a definitive sentence is pronounced or the trial is otherwise ended.

Wernz-Vidal,[99] in their introduction to attempts, state the pending of the litigation is terminated by way of a definitive sentence, against which no further appeal is granted,[100] by way of a compromise,[101] or by other means which usually end a trial. Beyond this no further specific means are indicated by these authors. They do, however, bring to the reader's attention that they have already considered, for the most part, how the pending of the litigation is ended in their previous consideration of the instance of the litigation.[102] In this discussion of the instance of the litigation they stated: the end of the instance of a lawsuit comes about in all the ways in which an end of the trial or controversy is reached.[103] Besides the ways in which the end of

[96] Cf. canon 1725.

[97] Canon 1732. Cf. Lega-Bartoccetti, *Commentarius*, II, 565 ff.; Wernz-Vidal, *Ius Canonicum*, VI, nn. 408 ff.; Coronata, *Institutiones*, II, n. 1259; Blat, *De Processibus*, nn. 229 ff.

[98] Cf. canons 1723, 1725, 1732, 1854, 1881, 1883, 1889, § 1.

[99] *Op. cit.*, VI, n. 569: "Litis pendentia in hac rubrica intelligebatur duratio controversiae in iudicium deductae, donec terminatur aut sententia definitiva, a qua ulterius non appellatur, aut transactione aliisque modis, quibus iudicium finiri solet."

[100] Cf. canons 1880 and 1902.

[101] Canons 1925-1932.

[102] *Op. cit.*, VI, n. 571: "Quot modis litis pendentia finiatur, iam maxima ex parte fuit expositum ubi actum est de litis instantia."

[103] *Op. cit.*, VI, n. 409: "... *finis* instantia fit omnibus modis quibus iudicium terminatur. Iudicium autem terminari potest pluribus modis:

a trial can be reached, the instance of the litigation can be interrupted or suspended;[104] it may also be terminated by way of peremption and renunciation.[105]

That the pending of the litigation does not necessarily end with the conclusion of the instance of the litigation is explained by Lega-Bartoccetti.[106] The instance reaches its conclusion through a definitive sentence. But as long as the sentence has not become irrevocably adjudged, the trial is not completely at an end. Therefore, a trial, in the broader sense, can consist of many instances—the first instance and the further instances of appeal. The instance, however, can be concluded prior to any definitive sentence by way of compromise or friendly settlement, by way of arbitration, and by way of renunciation or also through the destruction or loss of the litigious object, if it so ceases that its equivalent cannot, or indemnity for it need not, be substituted. In such ways as these, even if a trial is not understood as finished or defined apart from a definitive sentence, the instance, nevertheless is ended inasmuch as the controverted matter ceases.[107] The trial, as a trial, remains unfinished,

1°) terminatur modo ordinario per sententiam definitivam, quae in rem iudicatam transierit; 2°) si actore, post rei citationem, declarato contumaci ad normam can. 1850, reus obtineat a iudice absolutionem ab observatione iudicii (can. 1850, § 3); 3°) transactione inter partes inita, quae in qualibet iudicii parte est permissa (can. 1925, § 2); 4°) iureiurando litis decisorio (can. 1834); 5°) compromisso in arbitros (can. 1929)."

[104] Canons 1733-1735; 1856, § 1.

[105] Canons 1736-1740. Cf. Wernz-Vidal, *Ius Canonicum*, VI, n. 409.

[106] *Commentarius*, II, p. 565, n. 2.

[107] "Sane hisce modis, seu absque sententia definitiva iudicium non intelligitur absolvi nec definiri, sed terminum habet instantia quippe cessat res controversa. Videlicet iudicium remanet inabsolutum quia alia ratione habita est solutio quaestionis."—Lega-Bartoccetti, *loc. cit.* This statement seems misleading by reason of the choice of terminology, since *de facto* a trial can reach its conclusion by way of compromise, by way of arbitration, etc. Cf. Wernz-Vidal, *op. cit.*, VI, n. 409: "Iudicium autem terminari potest pluribus modis: ... 3°) transactione ... 5°) compromisso in arbitros"; n. 673: "... transactio aequiparatur sententiae iudiciali et habet vim rei iudicatae...." Cf.

since a solution of the question is had from another quarter.

Before passing on to a discussion of the means by which the pending of the litigation and the instance of the litigation become terminated, one must give some consideration to the interruption of the instance and its affect on attempts. Coronata defines the instance of the litigation as the prosecution of the suit in one and the same stage of a trial.[108] The actual litigation, such as the presentation of proofs and the performance of other judicial acts by the parties, will occur during the instance of the litigation.[109]

The interruption of the instance is accomplished when the prosecution of the suit (*exercitium actionis*) is brought to a standstill for one of these reasons: (1) if a litigating party dies, (2) if there is a change of his juridic status through insanity, through excommunication, or through any other circumstances which deprive him of the ability or the right to press his claim, and (3) if a party loses the office by reason of which he brought the suit to court.[110] Though a distinction can be made between an interruption allowed by law and a suspension of the instance,[111] the matter of

canons 1925, 1929, 1629, § 1. It is hoped that the author's thought is not essentially miscontrued by the writer's rendering of this passage.

[108] *Institutiones*, III, n. 1259: "Litis instantia est exercitium actionis in uno eodemque iudicii gradu."

[109] Wernz-Vidal, *Ius Canonicum*, VI, n. 409: "Instantia potest significare ipsam petitionem iudicialem; praesertim vero sumitur in significatione propria huius tituli pro actuali exercitatione seu *exercitio actionis* et 'complectitur omnes actus iudiciales ordinatos ad causam instruendam et definitiva sententia terminandam.'" Lega- Bartoccetti, *Commentarius*, II, 565: "Instantia est *exercitium actionis iudicialis*."

[110] Canon 1733. Si pars litigans moriatur aut statum mutet aut cessat ab officio cuius ratione agit: 1°. Causa nondum conclusa, instantia interrumpitur, donec heres defuncti aut successor litem instauret...." Cf. Lega-Bartoccetti, *Commentarius*, II, 566; Wernz-Vidal, *Ius Canonicum*, VI, n. 410: "...interrumpitur processus ratione mutationis, quae in alterutra parte aut in eius procuratore locum habet, et ex qua pars aut procurator inducuntur in impossibilitatem materialem vel legalem permanendi in iudicio."

[111] Wernz-Vidal, *loc. cit.*: "Porro *suspendi* dicunt processum propter

their effect upon the instance and on prejudicial attempts is the same; they do not disturb the pending of the litigation. Wernz-Vidal[112] note here that the Code makes no such distinction, though, in one sense, the instance in relation to the principal cause is suspended—not interrupted—by the adjudication of an incidental question. This fact is especially true if the incidental questions are of such a nature that they must be defined before the principal cause can go forward. Canon 1856, § 1, expressly states that the principal cause is regularly suspended when there is question of an attempt.

It is stated by Coronata that during the interruption of the instance provided by law[113] the pending of the litigation continues, that the instance cannot be ended by peremption, and that the judicial process cannot be further developed.[114] A prejudicial attempt, therefore, can be committed during the interruption of the instance, since the litigation continues to pend, until the instance perishes according to canon 1736 (peremption).

Canon 1732 is very succinct in its statement of the ways in which the instance of the litigation can be brought to an end.[115] It mentions particularly peremption and renunciation. It is evident, however, from the use of the words "*finis autem omnibus modis, quibus, iudicium terminatur*" that the listing of the ways specifically stated in the canon is demonstrative and not all-inclusive, especially since a

eventus, qui eius cursum impediunt, quique non dependent a statu, quem partes aut earum procuratores in iudicio habent." Cf. Lega-Bartoccetti, *op. cit.*, II, 566, art. 1, n. 1.

[112] *Op. cit.*, VI, n. 410, note 5. But see also can. 1736.

[113] Cf. canons 1733, 1735-1736.

[114] *Institutiones*, III, n. 1260: "Durante interruptione lis pendet, at instantia perimi nequit, nec processus evolvi potest." Cf. canon 1733, 1°. But see also can. 1736.

[115] "... finis autem omnibus modis, quibus iudicium terminatur, sed et antea non solum interrumpi, verum etiam finiri potest sive peremptione sive renunciatione." Cf. Wernz-Vidal, *Ius Canonicum*, VI, n. 409; Coronata, *Institutiones*, III, n. 1259.

definitive sentence is the more usual means whereby the instance becomes terminated.

1. Res Iudicata

A tribunal is well aware that a sentence pronounced by it is not altogether immune from possible error. This error may arise from the lack of a proper knowledge or even from a malicious intent. Thus, it is possible to envision a sentence that is not only invalid, but even unjust and injurious to the rights of the interested persons. Nevertheless it is necessary for a sentence to become so established according to law that the controversy is defined with a permanency and lastingness. If such a permanency were not provided for by the law, then the efforts of the court would often be in vain. The common good demands, furthermore, a judge who judges, yet is not judged. Otherwise appeals and other means of impugning the sentence, by being invoked incessantly, would prolong the controversy endlessly. This necessary quality of permanency and lastingness is given to a sentence by the law. Thus a sentence which fulfills the requirements prescribed in canon 1902 will become irrevocably adjudged (*res iudicata*).

However, by reason of the seriousness of the matter involved, the Code[116] makes an exception to the norm indicated in canon 1902, namely, causes regarding the status of persons never become irrevocably adjudged. The various forms of status most likely contemplated by canon 1903 are those which relate to marriage, to sacred orders, and to religious profession.[117]

Among the means which may terminate a controversy, the ones for which provision is made in canon 1902 are singularly important, since the litigious matter (*res litigiosa*) becomes irrevocably adjudged as these means obtain force. Therefore, in the treatment of the subject matter

[116] Canon 1903.

[117] Cf. Wernz-Vidal, *Ius Canonicum*, VI, n. 634; Noval, *De Iudiciis*, n. 675; Vermeersch-Creusen, *Epitome Iuris Canonici*, III, n. 245.

the writer will consider these means first, since a judicial process once opened tends to the natural and ordinary conclusion by way of a definitive sentence, which has or will become irrevocably adjudged.

The fact that a cause has become irrevocably adjudged can be viewed in two ways. Etymologically the words convey the notion that a controversy has been ended by way of a judicial definition. Since, however, a sentence is not practically definitive as long as it can be appealed to a court of higher instance, the meaning which is more proper to the subject matter of prejudicial attempts is that a sentence becomes irrevocably adjudged only when an appeal can no longer be interposed against it. It is in this last sense that the litigious matter must be understood as becoming a *res iudicata*, if the termination of the pending of the litigation is to be determined exactly.

The matter under litigation may become irrevocably adjudged in three ways: [118] a) by way of two concordant sentences; b) by way of a sentence which has not been appealed within the period granted for interposing an appeal (ten days computed as *tempus utile*),[119] or, if the invoked appeal has been abandoned by the appellate judge or court;[120] c) by way of definitive sentence from which no appeal is granted according to the norms of canon 1880. Thus, the instance of the litigation reaches its conclusion through the definitive sentence, but the pending of the litigation ceases when the sentence becomes irrevocably adjudged. Consequently, prejudicial attempts cannot any longer be committed once the pending litigation has come to an end.

a) *Two Concordant Sentences*

Two sentences in different stages of a trial are said to be concordant,[121] if the sentence of the court of higher in-

[118] Cf. Wernz-Vidal, *Ius Canonicum*, VI, n. 631 ff.; Coronata, *Institutiones*, III, nn. 1423 ff.

[119] Cf. canon 1881.

[120] Cf. canons 1883 and 1886.

[121] Cf. Lega-Bartoccetti, *Commentarius*, III, 2 ff.

stance confirms the sentence of the lower instance completely and in full. If the judge of the appeal, however, corrects a part of the sentence appealed, only the uncorrected part, provided that the parts of the sentence are separable, becomes irrevocably adjudged; this is so because of the conformity of the earlier sentence, at least partially, with the sentence later rendered on appeal.[122] Since canon 1880, 4°,[123] states that no appeal is granted from a sentence which has become irrevocably adjudged, that sentence, with regard to the part which is not subject to correction, cannot be appealed. Nevertheless, that part of the sentence which leaves room for a permissible correction can be appealed, since it has not yet become irrevocably adjudged by virtue of canon 1902, 1°. Finally, if in the third instance a concordant sentence is pronounced in regard to the corrected part of the sentence in question, then the litigious matter becomes completely and irrevocably adjudged, and the pending of the litigation is at an end.

b) *Failure to Interpose Appeal during the* TEMPUS UTILE

Canon 1881 grants ten days from the reception of the notice of the sentence as the available time (*tempus utile*)[124]

[122] Cf. Coronata, *Institutiones*, III, n. 1423.

[123] "Non est locus appellationi . . . 4°. A sententia quae in rem iudicatam transiit."

[124] Cf. Canon 35. The problem arises as to how the days within this period of "available time" are to be reckoned, especially when the interval of time, though once begun, is not actually continuous from one day to the next until the end is reached, but on the contrary suffers an interruption by reason of an impediment which proves to be a hindrance to the completion of the days assigned. Then again, how should the days thus impeded be computed and what standard are we to look to in order to determine such an "impeded" day which would not be included in the period of available time? The common opinion as advanced by Michiels (*Norma Generales Iuris Canonici*, II, 278) states that these impeded or unavailable days are to be reckoned *from day to day*. Consequently, a day which is impeded for a notable part must be juridically considered as completely impeded. This impeded day will be deleted from those days of available time and another day will be added to complete the number of days as-

for the interposing of an appeal. If an appeal is not made, the controversy becomes irrevocably adjudged and the pending of the litigation thereby ceases. Nevertheless, the prescriptions of canons 1885 and 1847 must be kept in mind.[125]

Canon 1885, § 1,[126] prescribes that if a litigant dies within the time granted for an appeal but before the appeal was interposed, or sustains a change in his status, or loses the office which empowered him to bring the suit, the sentence must be communicated to the heir or successor of this litigant, and the term designated by law for the appeal begins

signed. Michiels follows Dube (Arthur J., *The General Principles for the Reckoning of Time in Canon Law*, The Catholic University of America Canon Law Studies, n. 144, Washington, D.C.: The Catholic University of America Press, 1941, pp. 235-240) in this matter. Dube (*op. cit.*, p. 237) in discussing a day as impeded for a notable part gives a good indication of just how variable the "notableness" can be: "The solution of the problem appears as soon as one knows what constitutes an impediment of one day's duration. A day, in theory, consists of 24 hours reckoned continuously from midnight to midnight. However, when available time is considered, then a day consists de facto in the amount of time which one may actually use, and varies with the nature of the institute involved. Thus a day for the purpose of appealing lasts only as long as the court or chancery office is open. It is obvious that one cannot appeal at 2 A.M. If these offices are open from 9 A.M. to 5 P.M., only eight hours are available. If one is impeded during these eight hours it is clear that a full canonical day is rendered unavailing and that an extra day is to be added to the total of the continuous days originally granted." Michiels (*op. cit.*, II, pp. 277-278): "... ut autem determinetur quandonam agens per notabilem diei partem sit impeditus, non attendendus est dies theoretice consideratus, invariabiliter constans 24 horis, sed dies practice intellectus, talis scilicet qualis, attenta specifica natura instituti de quo in concreto agitur, ad jus exercendum vel prosequendum est de facto aptus, ita ut tempus utile revera moraliter sit computandum."

[125] Cf. Wernz-Vidal, *Ius Canonicum*, VI, n. 633.

[126] "Si casus de quo in can. 1733 contigerit intra terminum ad appellandum utilem sed antequam appellatio interposita sit, sententia debet iis quorum interest denuntiari eisque concessi intelliguntur termini a iure statuti a die denunctiationis computandi." Canon 1733.—"Si pars litigans moriatur aut statum mutet aut cesset ab officio cuius ratione agitur...."

to run for the person substituted from the day on which the notification was received.

Canon 1847 prescribes that, after a sentence has been pronounced, the person guilty of contempt of court may petition the judge who issued the sentence to reinstate him in the right of appeal (*beneficium restitutionis in integrum ad appellandum*).[127] This petition, however, must be made within three months from the day on which notice of the sentence was received.[128] If canon 1850, § 3, has been invoked and the defendant has been discharged from the petition of the plaintiff, it is evident that the pending of the litigation ceases. In this event the law interprets the plaintiff's contempt of court as a renunciation of his right to any further adjudication of the cause; whether or not he has recourse to the remedy afforded by canon 1847 at some future time will not affect the pending of the litigation which was originally set in motion by the plaintiff's petition, but which was terminated by the defendant's absolution from this very petition. If the right to appeal is granted to a person against whom such a sentence has been pronounced, then the duration of the pending of the litigation is governed by canons 1881, 1883, 1886 and 1902, 2°.[129]

c) *Definitive Sentence Admitting no Appeal*

A sentence is defined by the Code as the legitimate pronouncement by which a judge defines a cause submitted by the litigants for a judicial cognizance.[130] There are two

[127] Cf. also canons 1905-1907.

[128] Canon 1847—Post latam vero sententiam, contumax beneficium restitutionis in integrum ad appellandum ab ipso iudice qui eam tulit, petere potest, non ultra tamen trimestre ab ipsius sententiae intimatione, nisi agatur de causis quae non transeunt in rem iudicatam. Cf. canon 1903; also Wernz-Vidal, *Ius Canonicum,* VI, n. 637; Coronata, *Institutiones,* III, n. 1423.

[129] Wernz-Vidal (*Ius Canonicum,* VI, n. 558, 3°) state that the defendant who has been definitively discharged from the plaintiff's petition according to canon 1850, § 3, can lodge an *exceptio rei iudicatae,* if the plaintiff again proposes his petition in another instance.

[130] Canon 1868, § 1.—Legitima pronunciatio qua iudex causam a

kinds of sentences, i.e., the interlocutory sentence and the definitive sentence. Though canon 1868 makes no mention of the fact, the interlocutory sentence in turn allows for a twofold division, namely, the simple interlocutory sentence (*interlocutoria simplex*) and the interlocutory sentence with definitive force (*interlocutoria vim definitivae habens*).[131] A definitive sentence is one which defines and terminates the principal controvery of a trial;[132] whereas the interlocutory sentence is pronounced by the judge upon some controversy which arises after the beginning of the principal cause and before the definitive sentence.

Previous to the Code and before the Council of Trent (1545-1563) an appeal was permitted by Decretal Law[133] from every interlocutory sentence, provided only that it did not appear worthless and deceptive. The Council of Trent, however, put a limitation upon the right to appeal from an interlocutory sentence.[134] It prohibited an appeal from an interlocutory sentence, unless the sentence was an interlocutory sentence with definitive force, or one in which the injury to the innocent person could not be repaired by way of a definitive sentence or through an appeal from the definitive sentence.[135]

Lega-Bartoccetti discuss the possibility whether or not the last part of the prohibition of the Council[136] is to be in-

litigantibus propositam et iudiciali modo pertractatam definit, sententia est.

[131] Cf. canon 1880: "Non est locus appellationi: ....6° a iudicis decreto vel a sententia interlocutoria, quae non habeat vim definitivae, nisi cumuletur cum appellatione a sententia definitiva."

[132] Cf. Wernz-Vidal, *Ius Canonicum*, VI, n. 587; *supra*, page 23 ff.

[133] Cc. 12-19, X, *de appellationibus, recusationibus et relationibus*, II, 28.

[134] Sess. XXIV, *de ref.*, c. 20: "...nisi a definitiva vel a definitivae vim habente, et cuius gravamen per appellationem a definitiva reparari nequeat."

[135] Cf. sess. XIII, *de ref.*, c. 1; Wernz-Vidal, *Ius Canonicum*, VI, n. 587.

[136] Sess. XXIV, *de ref.*, c. 20: "...cuius gravamen per definitivam reparari nequeat."

cluded in the interpretation of canon 1880, 6°. Lega- Bartoccetti conclude that an appeal from a simple interlocutory sentence is not admissible by canon 1880, 6°, even though its purpose would be to repair an injury. The reason is that canon 1880, 6°, avoided using the phrase "*cuius gravamen per definitivam reparari nequeat,*" since it would practically allow an appeal as often as an appellant believed the injury imposed upon him could not be repaired by a definitive sentence.[137]

Against an interlocutory sentence there is, nevertheless, a remedy other than an appeal. This remedy is provided by canon 1841: before the principal cause is concluded, the judge can for a just reason correct or revoke the interlocutory sentence. He may do this on his own initiative (*ex officio*) after he has heard the parties, or at the request of one of the parties, provided he has given a hearing to his opponent. However, if the promoter of justice or the defender of the bond has taken part in the case, his opinion must be asked before the judge changes an interlocutory sentence.

The conclusion arrived at regarding the effect of an interlocutory sentence with reference to the question of prejudicial attempts committed against the respective incidental question is the following: (1) If it is a simple interlocutory sentence, then no appeal from it is granted by the Code, unless it is included with an appeal from the definitive sentence.[138] Since it is not possible to have an appeal from a simple interlocutory sentence, which would be independent of an appeal from the definitive sentence, the pending of the litigation will not be affected by such a sentence (*interlocutoria simplex*). In this event the pending of the litigation will continue until the trial itself is ended by means of a definitive sentence from which there is no further ap-

[137] *Commentarius,* II, p. 930, n. 3: "Iamvero ex iure nostro appellatio non admittitur, quia revera *vim non habet definitivae* interlocutoria excludens certam probationis speciem, et de tali gravamine fiet querelae caput in appellatione adversus definitivam."

[138] Cf. canon 1880, 6°.

peal,[139] or of a compromise,[140] or of peremption,[141] or of the other means discussed in the following pages.[142] (2) If it is an interlocutory sentence with a definitive force, then prejudicial attempts can be committed against the litigious matter, since the litigation continues to pend.[143]

An interlocutory sentence has definitive force if it brings about a loss which cannot be restored by means of a definitive sentence in the same instance; or if it is such that it requires the definitive sentence to be pronounced in a certain, determined sense.[144] Since an interlocutory sentence with definitive force is not excluded by canon 1880, 6°, from appeal, the litigation accordingly continues to pend upon its pronouncement. The pending of an appeal from such a sentence will be governed by canons 1881, 1883, 1886, 1889, 1854. Therefore, attempts are possible since the pending litigation has not come to a close.

Some examples of interlocutory sentences with definitive force are the following:[145] (1) an interlocutory sentence which denies an appeal or declares that it is deserted;[146] (2) that sentence by which the office of a judge ceases, i.e., if the judge pronounces himself incompetent;[147] (3) a sen-

[139] Cf. canon 1902, 3°.

[140] Cf. canon 1925.

[141] Cf. canon 1736.

[142] Cf. *infra*, pp. 93 ff.

[143] Cf. canons 1881, 1883, 1889, 1854.

[144] Wernz-Vidal, *Ius Canonicum*, VI, n. 606, 6°: "... Decretum vel sententia habet vim definitivate si damnum causat quod per sententiam definitivam reparari non possit, aut sit talis, ut efficiatur definitivam sententiam necessario determinato quodam sensu esse pronuntiandam"; n. 587: "... si ita praeiudicat negotio principali, ut alia sententia non iam sperari possit, appellatur *mixta* sive *vim definitivae habens.*" Cf. Coronata, *Institutiones*, III, n. 1394; also Roberti, *De Processibus*, I, n. 205 (I, 3).

[145] Cf. Reiffenstuel, *Ius Canonicum*, Lib. II, tit. 27, nn. 18-23; Wernz-Vidal, *Ius Canonicum*, VI, n. 606, p. 578, note 61; Lega-Bartoccetti, *Commentarius*, II, p. 930, nn. 4 f.

[146] Cf. Reiffenstuel, *op. cit.*, Lib. II, tit. 27, n. 18.

[147] Cf. canon 1610, § 3. Reiffenstuel, *ibid.*, n. 20: "Sententia interlocutoria, per quam expirat officium iudicis, dicitur habere vim diffi-

tence by which a peremptory exception is admitted or rejected;[148] (4) one which binds a party to give or do something, inasmuch as a definitive sentence in the same instance would not repair an injury already inflicted through the interlocutory sentence.[149]

Canon 1902, 3°, causes a matter under litigation to become irrevocably adjudged if the sentence pronounced is a single definitive sentence (*sententia definitiva unica*) from which no further appeal is granted according to canon 1880. Coronata[150] notes that in this event the object of controversy becomes irrevocably adjudged as soon as the definitive sentence has been published, so that there is no need of awaiting a lapse of the ten days normally allowed for an appeal. It is to be recalled here that simple interlocutory sentences can be corrected or revoked by the judge who pronounced them during the instance itself.[151] After a definitive sentence has been pronounced, however, these interlocutory sentences do not become irrevocably adjudged until the definitive sentence has itself become such.[152] Besides the cases of the litigious matter becoming irrevocably adjudged as given in canon 1902, others receive mention in the Code: (1) when the instance abates in consequence of a non-prosecution of the suit for a year upon appeal,[153]

nitivae. Sic accidit, quando iudex interloquendo pronuntiat se non esse competentem iudicem ('Iudicis enim existimare, an sua sit iurisdictio,'... [D. (5.1) 5]) quia sic interloquendo iam est functus officio suo...." Cf. also Reiffenstuel, *ibid.*, n. 21.

148 Cf. canon 1629, §1.—"Exceptiones peremptoriae, quae dicuntur *litis finitae*, veluti exceptio rei iudicatae, transactionis, etc...." Reiffenstuel, *ibid.*, n. 22. Wernz-Vidal (*Ius Canonicum*, VI, n. 257) speak of another division of peremptory exceptions other than those mentioned in can. 1629, § 1. This second division contemplates "simple peremptory exceptions." Examples of such exceptions are: "*exceptiones doli, metus, erroris ex contractu rescindibili.*"

149 Cf. Reiffenstuel, *ibid.*, n. 23.

150 *Institutiones*, III, n. 1423 (b, gamma).

151 Canon 1841.

152 Cf. Wernz-Vidal, *Ius Canonicum*, VI, n. 633; Coronata, *loc. cit.*

153 Canon 1736.

(2) when a renunciation of the instance has been made in an appeal by the plaintiff through the fact that he has not undertaken any further procedural act for the period of one year.[154]

In canon 1880 an appeal is denied in the following instances: (1) from the sentence of the Supreme Pontiff himself or the Apostolic Signatura;[155] (2) from the sentence of a judge who has been delegated by the Holy See to adjudicate a cause with the direction that no appeal is to be permitted (*appellatione remota*);[156] (3) from a sentence vitiated with an invalidating effect;[157] (4) from a sentence which has caused the litigious matter to become irrevocably adjudged;[158] (5) from a final and definitive sentence based on an oath taken for the purpose of reaching a decision in the litigated cause;[159] (6) from a decree of the judge or from an interlocutory sentence which is without definitive force, unless it is joined to an appeal from a definitive sentence;[160] (7) from a sentence in a cause which is to be adjudicated with the utmost of dispatch (*expeditissime*);[161] (8) from a sentence pronounced against a person guilty of contempt of court, as long as he

[154] Canons 1741; 1736.

[155] Canon 1556. Cf. also canons 218; 228, § 2; 2332.

[156] Cf. canons 203, § 1; 1557, § 3; 1558. The Holy See alone can insert this clause in an appointment of a delegate judge. Coronata (*Institutiones*, III, n. 1409) states that, though this clause is used, appeals which are expressly permitted by the law are not considered prohibited. However, if the clause actually prevents an appeal, other means, such as the plaint of nullity (*querela nullitatis*), a request made to the Holy Father (*supplicatio ad Romanum Pontificem*), and the petition for reinstatement in one's former condition or position (*restitutio in integrum*) can be used.

[157] Cf. canons 1892-1895. Further discussion of this is regard to the termination of the pending litigation will be found in subsequent paragraphs (*infra*, page 89-90).

[158] Cf. canon 1902.

[159] Cf. canons 1834-1836.

[160] Cf. Lega-Bartoccetti, *Commentarius*, II, 982; Wernz-Vidal, *Ius Canonicum*, VI, n. 606, 6°.

[161] Cf. canons 1616; 1709, § 3; 1856, § 2.

has not relinquished his obstinacy;[162] (9) from a sentence against a party who has expressly stated in writing that he has renounced his right to appeal.[163]

The pending litigation, therefore, will be terminated immediately upon the pronouncement of the following sentences: (a) a sentence of the Supreme Pontiff or of the Apostolic Signatura; (b) a sentence of a judge delegated by the Holy See to take cognizance of a cause with the provision that no appeal can be made from this sentence; (c) a sentence which has become irrevocably adjudged; (d) a definitive sentence based upon an oath accredited with a decisive force; (e) a sentence pronounced against a party who has expressly renounced the appeal in writing. In these divers situations the appeal is denied, and so also is the available time (*tempus utile*)[164] for an appeal, during which period there otherwise would continue the pending of the litigation, if an appeal were sustainable.[165] The four remaining situations which can involve the denial of an appeal[166] do not invariably cause the pending of the litigation to cease when the sentence or decree is pronounced.

Canon 1880, § 3, denies an appeal from a sentence vitiated with nullity. It must be concluded that a sentence vitiated with nullity does not *ipso facto* terminate the pending litigation or cause the litigious matter to become irrevocably adjudged. The reasons are the following. It is a principle of law that whatever is affected with nullity produces no effect.[167] Thus, a sentence which is null cannot become irrevocably adjudged.[168] An appeal is granted against a valid

[162] Cf. canon 1846-1847; 1843. *Infra*, see page 92.

[163] Cf. canons 1740-1741. Lega-Bartoccetti, *op. cit.*, II, 984 f., nn. 14-15.

[164] Cf. canons 1881, 1883.

[165] Cf. canon 1889.

[166] Canon 1880, 3°, 6°, 7°, 8°.

[167] "Sane quod nullum est nullum effectum producit." Cf. Lega-Bartoccetti, *Commentarius*, II, 981, n. 6; Wernz-Vidal, *Ius Canonicum*, VI, n. 615.

[168] Cf. canons 11; 1892-1893; 1917, § 1. Vermeersch-Creusen, *Epi-*

sentence only, not against an invalid one.[169] Since an appeal is not granted in this event, the extraordinary remedy of the plaint of nullity (*querela nullitatis*)[170] is offered by canon 1893 for irremediable nullity, and by canon 1895 for remediable nullity. If the sentence is vitiated with irremediable nullity,[171] the pending litigation will cease provided no procedural act, namely, the interposition of the plaint of nullity,[172] has been placed after such a sentence for two years in the first instance, or for one year in the second instance. This cessation of the pending of the litigation is brought about, therefore, by peremption or abatement.[173]

If it is a remediable nullity that is being considered,[174] the pending litigation will cease if the plaint of nullity has not been proposed within three months from the day of the publication of the sentence.[175] The pending litigation ceases in this event, since the terms established by law[176] have been allowed to elapse without the placing of the proper act which would naturally have caused the pending of the litigation to continue until the question of nullity was decided. Here is exemplified a peremptory term.[177]

The second situation which does not terminate the pending litigation, though an appeal is denied, obtains when a decree of a judge or an interlocutory sentence without definitive force has been issued.[178] A decree or interlocutory sen-

tome, III, n. 245 (2); Wernz, *Ius Decretalium*, V, n. 671; Lega, *De Iudiciis*, I, n. 698; Coronata, *Institutiones*, III, n. 1423 (b, gamma).

169 Canon 1880, 3°.

170 Cf. Wernz-Vidal, *op. cit.*, VI, nn. 614 ff.; Lega-Bartoccetti, *op. cit.*, II, 1015 ff.; Coronata, *op. cit.*, III, nn. 1417 ff.

171 Cf. canon 1892.

172 Canon 1893.

173 Cf. canon 1736.

174 Cf. canon 1894.

175 Canon 1895.

176 Cf. canons 1634-1635; 1854.

177 Cf. Roberti, *De Processibus*, I, n. 181 (I), 182 (I, 1).

178 Canon 1880, 6°.

tence may be corrected or revoked by the judge,[179] but this action must be placed before the definitive sentence, which will close the principal cause, is pronounced. It is evident, therefore, that the pending of the litigation continues after the pronouncement of a decree or a simple interlocutory sentence, since they define an incidental question and are anticipatory to the adjudication of the principal cause of which they are but a part.[180]

An appeal is not granted against a sentence in a cause which the law requires to be defined with the utmost of dispatch (*expeditissime*).[181] The Code enumerates three occasions which enjoin such prompt action. They are: (1) the exception of suspicion;[182] (2) the rejection of the bill of complaint (*libellus*),[183] and (3) the declaration of the nullity of a prejudicial attempt.[184] The exception of suspicion and the declaration of nullity of a prejudicial attempt are incidental questions, which by their definition are controversies which originate from or are occasioned by the principal cause.[185] After these incidental questions have been adjudged, the pending of the litigation will continue, since the principal cause is not yet closed by way of a definitive sentence. Thus the litigation continues to pend whether or not the principal cause is appealed,[186] provided only that the sentence is one which allows the making of an appeal. Otherwise the pending litigation may cease by such means as compromise (*transactio*, can. 1925), arbitration (can. 1929), decisive oath (can. 1834), and so forth, as will be discussed in the following pages.

As to the rejection of the bill of complaint, it is to be observed that its admittance or rejection is a part of the

179 Canon 1841.
180 Cf. canons 1837, 1840, 1841, 1868.
181 Canon 1880, 7°.
182 Canon 1616.
183 Canon 1709, § 3.
184 Canon 1856, § 2.
185 Lega, *De Iudiciis,* I, n. 536.
186 Cf. canons 1881, 1883, 1886, 1889, 1902.

introductory phase of a cause. There can be no question of the termination of the pending litigation in this event, since the pending of the litigation has not yet been begun by the intimation of the citation to the defendant.[187]

Canon 1880, 8°, denies an appeal from a sentence pronounced against a party who has failed to recede from his contempt of court. In regard to the duration of the pending of the litigation after this sentence, the contumacious party who is primarily to be considered is the plaintiff. The continuance of the pending litigation is governed in regard to the plantiff by canon 1850, § 3.[188] If the plaintiff is charged with contempt of court, he may recede from his contempt and reinstitute his suit in either of two ways. The method to be followed will depend on whether the plaintiff recedes from his obstinacy and takes the proper action either before or after the final sentence. Canon 1846 states that any conclusion and proofs offered by the plaintiff, when he has receded from his contempt and has appeared in court before the final sentence, must be admitted. In this event the litigation continues to pend, since no final sentence has been issued.[189]

After the pronouncement of the sentence[190] the plaintiff may request of the judge that the right of appeal be restored to him. Canon 1847 grants the plaintiff three months within which to request the right to appeal (*restitutio in integrum ad appellandum*). During these three months the litigation continues to pend. If the peremptory term[191] has elapsed and the plaintiff has failed to make this request to the judge who pronounced the sentence against him, the litigation ceases to pend.

In causes which concern personal status (marriage, ordination, etc.), there never eventuates a cause which becomes

[187] Canon 1725.

[188] Cf. *infra*, page 99.

[189] Cf. canons 1849-1850.

[190] Canon 1847.

[191] Cf. canon 1634, § 1; Roberti, *De Processibus*, I, n. 182 (I, 1), p. 452.

irrevocably adjudged.[192] Even in these causes, however, two concordant sentences, without of course excluding all possibility of an appeal or of a plain of nullity, have an influence upon the pending of the litigation. After two concordant sentences there can be no new instance in court, unless new facts, evidence or arguments are presented, which implies that the debates on the facts previously presented are closed. The time during which prejudicial attempts could be committed, namely, the pending litigation, will be governed according to canons 1987 and 1996.

In matrimonial causes, canon 1987[193] supposes that the defender of the bond may always appeal within ten days after two concordant sentences, and leaves the decision to appeal solely to the conscience of the defender. It is necessary to wait these ten days after the defender of the bond has been notified, so far as prejudicial attempts are concerned, for the defender to declare that he will not appeal, so that the litigation can be said to cease pending only after this term.[194]

2. *Transactio*[195]

Title XVIII of the Fourth Book of the Code[196] is divided into two chapters: Compromise or friendly agreement (*Transactio*) and Arbitration (*Compromissum in arbitros*). A compromise or settlement outside of court[197] is regarded

[192] Canon 1903. Cf. Wernz-Vidal, *Ius Canonicum,* VI, n. 634.

[193] Cf. Wernz-Vidal, *Ius Canonicum,* V, n. 703: "In his causis duplex sententia conformis id efficit, ut alterior proposito non debeat admitti, nisi novis prolatis iisdemque gravibus argumentis vel documentis (can. 1903)." Coronata, *Institutitiones,* III, n. 1500. S.C. de Sacramentis, instr., *Provida Mater,* 15 aug. 1936, Art. 221—*AAS,* XXVIII (1936), 357.

[194] Cf. canon 35. The time under consideration here is available time (*tempus utile*).

[195] Canons 1925-1928.

[196] *De modis evitandi iudicium contentiosum.*

[197] Blat (*De Processibus,* n. 230) speaks of the "*compositio seu concordia,*" which is rather the effect of compromise. Cf. canon 1928, § 1. See also Coronata, *Institutiones,* III, n. 1259; Wernz-Vidal, *Ius Canonicum,* VI, nn. 354 ff.; Beste, *Introductio,* pp. 814, 841.

by the Code as a very desirable[198] means to be invoked, in order to avoid litigation among the faithful. Canon 1925 directs that the judge shall exhort the parties to reach a settlement, if any hope of a friendly agreement is had when a civil controversy over some private matter of theirs has arisen and has been brought into court for adjudication. The judge may admonish the parties before they are summoned to court, or when they appear in court for the first time, or, finally, at any time that he deems it more opportune and effective for suggesting the settlement.[199]

Compromise may be understood in two senses. In the broad sense, it is any friendly or peaceful agreement between the litigants. In the strict sense, which is the meaning employed for it in canon 1925, it is an onerous contract whereby the parties mutually give, retain or promise something in regard to the doubtful matter or controversy. Their purpose is to put an end to the controversy already begun, but not yet finished, or to prevent a controversy which perhaps may arise.[200] By reason of its effect the settlement (*transactio*) is designated as a friendly agreement (*compositio amicabilis*).[201] Sometimes the words *transactio, con-*

[198] Canon 1925, § 1: *"valde optandum."*

[199] Canon 1925, § 2.—Huic officio iudex satisfacere poterit sive antequam partes in iudicium vocentur, sive cum primum iudicio steterint, sive denique quocumque tempore et efficacius et opportunius id tentari posse existimaverit.

[200] Cf. Wernz-Vidal, *Ius Canonicum,* VI, n. 664. It will suffice to give here the essentials of *transactio* as determined by Beste (*Introductio,* p. 841): "... 1. habilitas paciscentium ex parte subiecti et ideo qui de subiecta aliqua materia contrahendi est incapax neque in eadem transigere valet; 2. res incerta vel controversa et transactionis ineundae capax ex parte obiecti, secus enim transigens sine titulo sibi appropriat rem alienam aut de materia vetita transigit; 3. pactio non gratuita sed onerosa ex parte actus, qua aliquid pretio aestimabile hinc inde remittitur." For a further discussion as to the persons capable of compromise, its object, form, time, etc., see the various authors.

[201] Cf. canon 1928, § 1.

cordia and *amicabilis composito* are used without differentiation.[202]

The importance of the friendly settlement here is its effect on the pending of the litigation, and accordingly on prejudicial attempts. It is the concerted opinion of the authors that a settlement or compromise is the equivalent of a judicial sentence and thus gives rise to an irrevocable adjudication.[203] Since the judge may urge this settlement at any time during the trial, it follows that, if the parties do come to an agreement during the controversy, then the litigation ceases to pend.[204] Thereupon there is no further possibility of the committing of prejudicial attempts against the litigious matter.[205]

3. *Compromissum in Arbitros*[206]

In order to avoid a judicial litigation the parties are permitted by the law to enter into an agreement by which the controversy is committed to the judgment of one or more persons. These persons are to decide the question according to law or are directed to determine the matter according to the rules of equity. If the procedure follows legal

[202] Cf. Lega-Bartoccetti, *Commentarius*, III, p. 121, n. 2; Blat, *Commentarium*, Lib. IV, n. 230.

[203] Wernz-Vidal, *Ius Canonicum*, VI, n. 673: "Nam transactio aequiparatur sententiae iudiciali et habet vim rei iudicatae." *ibid.*, n. 409, note 2: "... vere finitur iudicium, nam transactio habet vim rei iudicatae." Cf. Lega-Bartoccetti, *Commentarius*, III, p. 129, n. 10; Cappello, *Summa Iuris Canonici*, III, n. 360; Coronata, *Institutiones*, III, n. 1446.

[204] Canon 1629.

[205] This important observation is made by Wernz-Vidal (*op. cit.*, VI, n. 673, note 71): "Attamen nota rem iudicatam et transactionem non in omnibus convenire. Id autem ex eo quoque solum patet, quod transactio contractus est, non autem res iudicata et quod haec non possit de nullitate impugnari, transactio autem possit ex omnibus illis vitiis quibus ceterae pactiones impugnantur. Quare transactio rei iudicatae non aequiparatur, nisi restrictive ad punctum controversiae, super quo transactum est, ita ut utraque pariter impediat ne quaestio semel decisa iterum in controversiam possit adduci."

[206] Canons 1929-1932.

norms, these persons are called arbiters in law (*arbitri*); if the matters are expedited simply along equitable lines, these persons are called arbiters in equity (*arbitratores*).[207]

The distinction between arbiters in law and arbiters in equity comes to us by way of the pre-Code law. Wernz-Vidal[208] explain the difference as follows. An arbiter in law, in the strict sense, is a person who takes cognizance of the controverted matter after the manner of a judge. He defines the controversy by means of a sentence or *laudam*,[209] which the parties must observe, if they have previously agreed to accept the judgment of the arbiter in law. On the other hand, an arbiter in equity is one who decides a cause by the consent of the parties without a judicial trial. In adjudicating the controversy, he brings the charges to an end, estimates prices, costs, profit and loss. Then he pronounces judgment upon the matter. Such arbitration is a species of friendly settlement (*amicabilis compositio*). Thus the arbiter in equity can be likened to a mediator or a conciliator, who can be constituted either by public authority or by the free agreement of the parties.[210]

Arbiters in pre-Code law were such either by a necessitating law (necessary arbiters) or by optional deputation (voluntary arbiters). But, as Coronata observes,[211] this division is of no practical import to us any longer. In the Code, arbiters are always voluntary arbiters (*compromissarii*) and possess no public authority, since they are chosen not by the law as were the necessary arbiters (*arbitri iuris seu necessarii*), but by the parties themselves.

Once the judgment (*laudam seu arbitrium*) of the arbiters has been pronounced, the pending of the litigation is

[207] Canon 1929.

[208] *Ius Canonicum*, VI, n. 677. Cf. also Lega-Bartoccetti, *op. cit.*, III, p. 135, nn. 7 ff.; Coronata, *op. cit.*, III, n. 1447.

[209] Lega-Bartoccetti, *op. cit.*, III, p. 136, n. 7: "... sententia vero arbitrorum *arbitrium* seu *laudum* dicitur. Etenim *laudare* idem est ac *iudicare* in documentis medii aevii, veluti in *libris Feudorum*."

[210] Wernz-Vidal, *loc. cit.*

[211] *Institutiones*, III, n. 1447.

brought to a close, if this judgment is expressly accepted by the parties. Otherwise, if the judgment is accepted tacitly through a silence of ten days, the pending litigation is then terminated.[212]

4. *Iusiurandum Decisorium*[213]

An oath which entails a decision is one which one party proposes to the other party of a trial with the effect that by mutual agreement the controversy becomes settled by it.[214] According to canon 1834, the oath may be taken by either party, not only before the controversy has begun in court, but also during the pending litigation.[215] Moreover, at any time or stage in the cause, one party, with the approval of the judge, may propose an oath to the other, under the condition that the question,[216] either the principal cause itself or some incidental question, may be considered set-

[212] Wernz-Vidal, *Ius Canonicum,* VI, n. 687: "...At ex arbitrio homologato, sive approbato expresse aut tacite per silentium decem dierum, concessa erat exceptio et actio in factum tanquam de re iudicata coram iudice ordinario, et arbitrium indistincte ratum haberi debebat et executioni mandari..."; *ibid.*, n. 688: "...tamen *a laudo arbitrorum compromissariorum* appellari non potest, quia litigatores sponte elegerunt arbitros sibique damnum tribuere debent."

[213] Canon 1834, § 1.—Non solum ante initam litem partes convenire possunt ut controversia per iusiurandum ab alterutra praestandum transigendo dirimatur, sed pendente quoque lite et in quolibet eius momento et statu, altera pars potest, iudice probante, alteri iusiurandum deferre, ea conditione ut quaestio sive principalis sive incidens, secundum iusiurandum decisa habeatur.

[214] Wernz-Vidal, *Ius Canonicum,* VI, n. 541: "Iuramentum decisorium est illud iuramentum, quod una pars alteri defert ea lege, ut ex eo controversia decisa habeatur." Cf. Coronata, *Institutiones,* III, nn. 1366-1368.

[215] Coronata, *op. cit.,* III, n. 1366: "Dicitur in hoc can. 1834 in quolibet litis momento et statu deferri posse iusiurandum iudiciale—quod intelligendum est etiam de periodo appellationis aut de periodo post latam definitivam sententiam ante appellationem."

[216] Roberti, *De Processibus,* I, n. 33: "Quaestio ius controversum simpliciter indicat."

tled according to the oath. The conditions for the taking of the oath are delineated in canon 1835.[217]

It is evident that canon 1834 permits two different oaths, namely, the judicial and extrajudicial decision-entailing oath.[218] There is this difference, however, between the two: the judicial oath presupposes the approval of the judge and is executed in the trial. Beste[219] points out that the decision-entailing oath is essentially a species of compromise and is likened to it.

The effect of this oath upon the pending litigation is the following: it terminates the trial,[220] and therefore also the pending litigation, if the oath was taken with reference to the disputed question of the judicial controversy itself. This would not be the case if the oath contemplated simply an incidental question, since, though the incidental cause is ended by it, the principal cause still remains.[221]

Wernz-Vidal[222] made the following observation on the decision-entailing oath. The oath must be made before the judge of the cause and in the presence of the other party. After this requirement has been fulfilled, this effect follows: the question[223] contained in the formula of the oath is set-

[217] Cf. Wernz-Vidal, *op. cit.*, VI, n. 542; Cappello, *Summa Iuris Canonici*, III, n. 286.

[218] Cf. Wernz-Vidal, *loc. cit.;* Coronata, *op. cit.*, III, n. 1366.

[219] *Introductio*, p. 827: "Iuramentum decisorium essentia sua est species transactionis eique aequiparatur, cum semper inclusam habeat aliquam renuntiationem et acquisitionem saltem quoad modum agendi, et proinde omnibus regulis transactionis obnoxium manet." Cf. canons 1925-1928.

[220] Cf. canon 1629, § 1.

[221] Wernz-Vidal, *Ius Canonicum*, VI, n. 409, note 2: "...finitur iudicium...4°, si iusiurandum praestetur circa id quod constituit punctum controversiae, non si praestetur circa causam incidentalem, qua causa incidentali perempta adhuc manet instantia causae principalis"; *ibid.*, n. 541: "Per se etiam patet iuramentum habere posse pro obiecto integrum litis obiectum vel aliquem dumtaxat articulum vel incidentalem causam." Coronata, *op. cit.*, III, n. 1366.

[222] *Op. cit.*, VI, n. 543.

[223] Coronata, *Institutiones*, III, n. 1368: "Ut autem revera finis

tled in the same manner as though a cession or settlement in court (*transactio*) had taken place.[224] The judge then confirms what has already been decided by the decision-entailing oath. If a sentence is based on such an oath, there can be no appeal from it by reason of canon 1880, 5°. The sentence then becomes irrevocably adjudged. It is, therefore, seen that the pending litigation ceases once the oath has been taken. If the sentence is based upon the oath, the ten days for making an appeal are not granted.[225] If this oath, however, is taken after the sentence has been pronounced, either during the ten days which are granted by canon 1881 for the interposing of an appeal, or during the appeal itself (cf. cans. 1883, 1886, 1889), the pending of the litigation ceases.[226]

5. *Termination of the "Litis Pendentia" according to Canon 1850, § 3.*

Upon a judicial declaration that the plaintiff is guilty of contempt of court,[227] the defendant has the right to petition either that he be enabled to depart freely from the trial, or that all the acts undertaken to that time be declared null, or that he be definitively discharged from the petition of the plantiff, or that the trial, even though the plaintiff is absent, be conducted to the end.[228] In the discussion of this

quaestionis habeatur, requiritur ut iusiurandum decisorium post adversarii delationem praestitutum sit; alioquin sesponte ad illud praestandum offerens se suspectum reddit."

[224] Cf. canons 1836, § 2; 1925-1928.

[225] Cf. canon 1880, 5°; 1629, § 1. Coronata, *Institutiones*, III, n. 1368: "Iureiurando decisorio lis finitur absolute, ita ut contra sententiam latam vi huius iurisiurandi appellatio non detur et ipsa sententia vim habeat rei iudicatae."

[226] Canon 1834, § 1.—"Non solum ante initam litem partes convenire possunt ut controversia per iusiurandum ab alterutra praestandum transigendo dirimatur,..."

[227] Cf. canon 1844, § 1; and canons 1849-1850.

[228] Canon 1850, § 3.—Reus autem exinde ius habet petendi ut vel libere possit a iudicio abire, vel nulla habeantur omnia eo usque gesta, vel definitive ipse absolvatur a petitione actoris, vel iudcium, absente quoque actore, ad finem adducatur.

canon, it is to be supposed that the plaintiff does not recede from his obstinacy during the pending of the litigation,[229] for otherwise there would be no question that the pending litigation has been ended according to canon 1850, § 3. It is presumed that the plaintiff, therefore, continues steadfast in his contempt of court, at least until after one or the other of the indicated remedies is employed by the defendant.

One of the effects of the declaration of contumacy (contempt of court) in regard to the plaintiff is the loss of his right to continue prosecuting the judicial instance.[230] This right is considered as having been renounced by the plaintiff. The loss of this right does not become permanent through the sole declaration of contumacy. The plaintiff may, therefore, urge the adjudication of his action by reestablishing the judicial instance anew according to canon 1846, unless the suit has abated meanwhile in consequence of other causes, e.g., prescription.

The defendant possesses by virtue of canon 1850, § 3, the four remedies stated above. These he may invoke against a plaintiff guilty of contempt of court. The pending of the litigation can be affected by each of these remedies. In this event there is question of the termination of the pending litigation on motion of the defendant alone; whether or not the plaintiff may at another time move to have the judicial instance reinstated is a matter beyond the scope of this discussion.[231] The defendant's effectual use of any of these remedies will cause the pending of the litigation to cease as the prescriptions of this canon are fulfilled.

If the defendant petitions the judge to be allowed to depart freely from the trial, he equivalently requests the judge to annul or rescind the juridic effect of the citation.[232] The authors speak of this rescission of the citation as the "*cir-*

[229] Cf. canons 1846, 1849.

[230] Canon 1850, § 1.

[231] Cf. Lega-Bartoccetti, *Commentarius*, II, p. 881, n. 9.

[232] Cf. canon 1725.

cumductum edictum citationis."[233] Since the pending of the litigation arises from the citation, it ceases once the citation loses its juridic force through a rescission.

In the first remedy, the plaintiff is looked upon as having become guilty of contempt of court soon after the trial has begun. The second remedy granted to the defendant indicates that the trial has progressed beyond its initial stage before the plaintiff is declared contumacious, since canon 1850, § 3, makes mention of the annulment (rescission) of all the procedural acts undertaken up to the time when the plaintiff has been pronounced contumacious. The defendant requests, in effect, that he be absolved from the observance of the trial.[234] This absolution from the observance of the trial is brought about by the declaration of the judge that all the acts in this instance are rescinded and thus are null and void. Among the procedural acts which are rescinded through the use of this remedy is the citation. Thus the litigation ceases to pend, since the ruling contained in canon 1725 is no longer in effect or applicable.

The third remedy is operative when the defendant requests that he be definitively absolved from the petition of the plaintiff, so that the plaintiff may not be heard again in the same matter, and, if the plaintiff should wish to resume the trial, this must be denied him by way of an exception of irrevocable adjudication (*exceptio rei iudicatae*).[235] In this matter, the termination of the pending litigation together with the incidence of the irrevocable adjudication is governed by canon 1847.[236] The litigation will continue

[233] D. (5. 1) 73; (40. 12) 27; (49. 1) 22. Cf. Wernz-Vidal, *Ius Canonicum,* VI, n. 558 (1°); Lega-Bartoccetti, *op. cit.,* II, p. 881, n. 8; Noval, *De Iudiciis,* n. 595; Coronata, *Institutiones,* III, n. 1380.

[234] Cf. Wernz-Vidal, *op. cit.,* VI, n. 558 (2°); Lega-Bartoccetti, *op. cit.,* II, p. 881, n. 9; Noval, *loc. cit.;* Coronata, *loc. cit.*

[235] Cf. canon 1629, § 1. Coronata, *op. cit.,* III, n. 1380. Noval, *loc. cit.;* Wernz-Vidal, *op. cit.,* VI, n. 558 (3°).

[236] Cf. canon 1849. Cf. also Feeney, *Restitutio in Integrum,* The Catholic University of America Canon Law Studies, n. 129 (Washington, D.C.: The Catholic University of America Press, 1941), pp. 143-145.

to pend for three months after the defendant is definitively absolved from the plaintiff's petition. If the plaintiff does not have recourse to the option made available for him in canon 1847, the litigation will cease to pend after the lapse of three months, since the term assigned by the Code is a peremptory term.[237] If in accord with canon 1847 the plaintiff is granted the right to appeal, then the continuance of the pending litigation is determined according to the canons on appeals.[238]

The fourth remedy granted in canon 1850, § 3, enables the defendant to petition the court that the definitive sentence be pronounced in his own behalf. If this remedy is resorted to, it is prescribed by the Code that the trial is to be conducted to the end (*ad finem*). Wernz-Vidal[239] observed that the judge may not assign the controverted matter to the defendant by way of a definitive sentence, unless he has proved that the litigious matter legitimately belongs to him. The burden of proof rests with the defendant. Upon the pronouncement of the definitive sentence in favor of the defendant, the duration of the pending of the litigation is again governed by canon 1847. The litigation will continue to pend during the three months granted to the plaintiff to request the right to interpose an appeal. If this peremptory term is allowed to lapse, either with the denial of the petition[240] or apart from the plaintiff's prosecution,

[237] Cf. canon 1634, § 1; Roberti, *De Processibus*, I, n. 182 (I, 1).

[238] Cf. canons 1881, 1883, 1886, 1889, 1902, 2°.

[239] *Ius Canonicum*, VI, n. 558 (3°).

[240] Cf. canon 1841. An incidental question is raised (can. 1837). Its rejection is a pronouncement with the force of a definitive sentence, because it impedes an appeal on its merits, and hence tends virtually to become irrevocably adjudged according to can. 1902, 2°. Hence an appeal is admissible to the plaintiff on the basis of can. 1709, § 3, and according to can. 1880, 6°. A confirmation or reversal on this appeal is final upon the incidental question (cf. canon 1709, § 3). If a confirmation, there is an irrevocable adjudication on the question according to can. 1902, 1°, and there is no further appeal (cf. canon 1880, 7°). Thus the pending litigation in question follows the rules of an appeal on the basis of can. 1709, § 3, and can. 1837. But the

the litigation immediately ceases to pend; otherwise it will continue according to the rules of appeal.

6. *Peremptio*

Peremption of the judicial instance[241] is the expression used by the Code in designation of the juridical fact that a trial has ceased to pend, if no procedural act has been placed in a court of first instance for two years, or in a court of appeal for one year, provided that no impediment hindered the act from taking place. Blat[242] noted that, since judges and tribunals are admonished to see to the expeditious handling of all causes that are brought to them for adjudication, with a limit of two years set for a cause in first instance, and of one year for a cause in second instance,[243] equity demands that the parties also should be bound to the same diligence. Canon 1736, it has been seen, actually does exact from the parties a similar carefulness.

Coronata divides the impediments of peremption into public and private impediments. Public impediments such as war, epidemics, etc., must be recognized by the judge as a general rule. If the impediment is private, as in sickness, in a prolonged absence, etc., it is left to the prudent discretion of the judge whether to accept it or to reject it.[244]

Peremption obtains force by the law itself (*ipso iure*). Therefore it is not necessary that the party or promoter of justice submit a petition, nor that the judge decree it.[245] It is effective against minors and those who are likened to minors in ecclesiastical causes.[246]

three-month period indicated in can. 1847 remains intact, if still current, for the effect of can. 1841, since there is an interlocutory pronouncement.

241 Canons 1736-1739. Reg. 25, R.J. in VI°: "Mora sua cuilibet est nociva."

242 *Commentarium,* Lib. IV, n. 234.

243 Canon 1620.

244 *Institutiones,* III, n. 1262.

245 Blat, *Commentarium,* Lib. IV, n. 235. Cf. Wernz-Vidal, *Ius Canonicum,* VI, n. 413.

246 Canon 1737. See canon 100, § 1: "personae morales sive colle-

As previously mentioned[247] there is difficulty in determining what time one can look to as marking the beginning of the peremption, and hence also the basis upon which its determination is to be computed. If there is any doubt regarding the termination of the time interval (*terminus ad quem*), then another difficulty will arise in determining whether a prejudicial attempt was committed before or after the instance was abated.

In computing the time element of the termination of peremption, two aspects can be considered: a) as it is to be reckoned from the placing of the last *procedural* act to the two years in first instance and one year in second instance,[248] or b) as it is to be computed according to the rules governing the computation of time in the Code.[249]

Lega-Bartoccetti discuss here the question whether the term (*terminus a quo*) of peremption begins with the citation, if it alone has taken place, or is to be computed solely from the beginning of the joinder of issue.[250] The reason for this doubt is twofold. In the law of Justinian, namely, the *Lex Properandum*, it was decreed that civil causes were to be prolonged not more than three years *after* the joinder of issue had taken place. But in the Code[251] the beginning of peremption seems to commence with the joinder of issue. The term (*terminus a quo*) of peremption should be considered as having begun with the citation, once it has been intimated to the defendant. The reason for this is that the citation, if it is properly served, is a procedural act, and canon 1738 states that the acts of the *process* are terminated by peremption. Unless the citation and its intimation (both together constitute the *actus citationis*)[252] are included in

giales sive non collegiales"; and canon 1648, § 1: "ii, qui rationis usu destituti sunt." Cf. also canon 88, § 3.

[247] Cf. *supra*, pp. 73 ff.

[248] Lega-Bartoccetti, *Commentarius*, II, 588 f.

[249] Canons 31-35.

[250] *Op. cit.*, II, 588 f.

[251] Canon 1732.

[252] Cf. Lega-Bartoccetti, *Commentarius*, II, p. 537.

our interpretation of the matter as a proper procedural act, it would not be abated by peremption. Canon 1738 should not prove to be an insurmountable obstacle here, since, though the instance begins properly and formally with the joinder of issue, the instance can also be said to comprehend—virtually and effectively—the citation, which is the basis and foundation of the instance of the litigation. Therefore peremption can be considered as potentially beginning with the serving of the summons (citation) upon the defendant.[253] Thus the terms within which a prejudicial attempt can be committed, if the joinder of issue has not taken place, are the beginning of the pending litigation[254] and the abatement of the instance by peremption.[255]

7. *Renuntiatio*

Canon 1740, § 1, established it as a norm that in any stage and in any judicial instance attending a trial or a litigation the plaintiff may renounce the istance. Moreover, the plaintiff and the defendant may renounce all or simply some of the acts of the process. The effects of the renunciation are the same as those of the peremption in regard to the acts renounced, but only after the renunciation has been accepted by the judge.[256]

In this canon and in canon 1741, the *express* character is the factor which primarily differentiates a renunciation from a peremption. Peremption obtains force *ipso iure*, but is founded upon the presumed or tacit renunciation of the instance by one of the parties.[257]

According to Coronata, a distinction is to be made between the renunciation of the instance and the renunciation of the litigation and the acts of the process. The renunciation of the litigation can always take place, and by it the

[253] The time to be employed in the computation is available time (*tempus utile*). Cf. Lega-Bartoccetti, *op. cit.*, II, p. 589, n. 3.

[254] Canon 1725, 5°.

[255] Canon 1736.

[256] Cf. canons 1738, 1739, 1741.

[257] Lega-Bartoccetti, *Commentarius*, II, 597.

suit (*actio*), the instance, and also the procedural acts (*actus*) are renounced. Renunciation of the instance implies the renunciation of the actual prosecution of the trial and of the judicial action, which latter, nevertheless, can be instituted again before the same judge or another who is competent.[258] Therefore, once the instance is renounced according to the prescriptions of the law, the litigation ceases to pend.

The renunciation of the acts does not imply that the suit or its instance has been renounced; it implies this for only particular judicial acts. Meanwhile the remaining acts not specified as well as the instance itself retain their *status quo*.[259] Thus, since the renunciation of an act or of a determined number of acts does not inherently (*per se*) affect the instance itself, the litigation continues to pend, and any prejudicial attempts committed after this renunciation will be null *ipso iure*. Wernz-Vidal state that one party apart from the other can renounce only such acts as have been undertaken in behalf of his own petition, provided of course that no prejudice is inflicted on the other litigant.[260] Before the renunciation of the instance or of an act becomes effective, five conditions must be met. They are: a) the renunciation must be made in writing, b) the party or his procurator, who needs a special mandate, must sign the renunciation; c) it must be communicated to the other party; d) it must be accepted by this party (at least not opposed by him); and e) it must be permitted by the judge.[261]

[258] *Institutiones*, III, n. 1265. Lega-Bartoccetti (*op. cit.*, II, p. 601, n. 10) hold that the citation and the joinder of issue can both be renounced: "Sane renunciatio ait can. 1740 fieri potest in quocumque statu iudicii, seu cum nonnulli tantum actus, ut ecce citatio tantum litis contestatio locum habuerunt."

[259] Canon 1740, § 1.

[260] *Ius Canonicum*, VI, n. 415: "Unusquisque litigans seorsim ab alio non potest renunciare nisi actis ad propriam petitionem positis et sine alterius partis praeiudicio."

[261] Canon 1740, § 2.

8. *Extinctio Actionis*[262]

During the pending of the litigation, if the suit (*actio*) itself is quashed, then the litigation likewise ceases to pend. In this matter of the quashing of suits, canons 1701-1705 point to some of the situations in which the suit becomes terminated.

Canon 1701 prescribes: In contentious causes both real and personal judicial suits become quashed through the agency of prescription according to the norms of canons 1508-1512; however, suits which concern the status of persons never become extinguished. Prescription, nevertheless, cannot be one of the means by which the suit can be quashed during the pending litigation. The reason for this statement is to be found in canon 1725, 4°.[263] Consequently, once the citation has been legitimately made, prescription is interrupted.[264] It will not affect the judicial suit, then, during

[262] Wernz-Vidal, *Ius Canonicum,* VI, n. 359: "Extinctio actionis [est] resolutio iuris reum in determinata causa conveniendi.... Quae extinctio actionis omnino est distinguenda ab extinctione vel peremptione instantiae; nam instantia est exercitium actionis in determinato processu iudiciali, quo finito per instantiae peremptionem quin intercesserit firma sententia rem iudicatam inducens, actio potest in alio processu de novo instaurando promoveri, nisi aliunde ipsa actio fuerit extincta." Cf. also Lega-Bartoccetti, *Commentarius,* II, p. 566, n. 2; Roberti, *De Processibus,* I, nn. 255 ff.

[263] "Cum citatio legitime peracta fuerit aut partes sponte in iudicium venerit... 4°. Interrumpitur praescriptio, nisi aliud cautum sit, ad normam can. 1508." In consequence of canon 1508 the statutes of the civil law of a nation are generally accepted by the ecclesiastical court.

[264] Wernz-Vadal, *Ius Canonicum,* VI, n. 393: "... Ergo praescriptio per citationem non interrumpitur *naturaliter,* i.e., ex eo quod deficiat aliqua ex conditionibus requisitis (v.gr. quod mala fides supervenit, titulus resolvitur, possessio amittitur); sed interrumpitur *civiliter* ex edispositione iuris, quae rem reddit iuridice litigiosam et hac conditione durante impraescriptibilem ... ;" Roberti, *De Processibus* (4. ed.), I, n. 255 (II, 3, b): "Praescriptio interrumpitur naturaliter et civiliter ... civiliter citatione (c. 1725, 4°; CproEOdeIu c. 247, 4°) aut aliis actibus quibus a lege effectus interrumpendi praescriptionem attributus sit. Praescriptio interrupta integrum cursum ab initio peragere debet."

the pending of the litigation. Therefore prescription cannot terminate the pending litigation.

There are, however, means which will so affect the judicial suit after the citation has been made, that the litigation will cease to pend as a consequence. Since most of these means are apparent, and some have already been discussed, because they have been given special consideration by the Code,[265] it will not be necessary to give them detailed consideration here. These means in summary are: (1) the payment of the debt; (2) a condonation; (3) at times the death of one of the litigants (cf. can. 1702, concerning criminal suits); (4) the merging of plaintiff and defendant in one and the same person; (5) the loss or destruction of the litigious object, if no one is bound to restore its equivalent or to make indemnification for it; (6) full compensation; (7) complete renunciation, and (8) settlement.[266]

It is to be noted that the renunciation is to be made in writing.[267] The compromise that is entered into must comply with the civil statutes of the place where the settlement is undertaken.[268] Therefore, to forestall any attempts of the plaintiff to prosecute his suit in court, when the suit has already been quashed by such means as the payment of the debt or the granting of a condonation, it seems a point of proper discretion to have a legal document drawn up in proof of that fact.

Article 2. The Perpetrator of the *Attentatum*

The Code leaves no doubt as to who may be considered as the cause of the prejudicial attempt. There are but three possibilities to be enumerated: one or the other of the parties of the trial or also the judge of the cause. The prejudicial attempt may, therefore, be committed by one party against the other (plaintiff against defenant; defendant

[265] Cf. canon 1925, "settlement;" canon 1740, "renunciation." Cf. *supra*, pp. 93 and 105 respectively.

[266] Cf. Roberti, *loc. cit.;* Coronata, *Institutiones*, III, n. 1231.

[267] Cf. canon 1740, § 2.

[268] Cf. canon 1926; 1927-28.

against plaintiff) or by the judge against one or both of the parties.[269]

In the pre-Code law it was discussed among the authors whether or not a third person could commit a prejudicial attempt which would have to yield to the *remedium attentati.* Jordanus[270] was of the opinion that a procurator could commit a prejudicial attempt only if he had a special mandate from the party to act, and not if the mandate was simply a general one.

The Code does not consider attempts committed by other persons than the parties in the cause or the judge. Woywod (1880-1941)[271] pointed out that "unless they [others] interfere with the rights of the party at the instigation of a party or of the judge (in which case it would be the same as though the latter were themselves guilty of the attempt), the injury which is done to a party by a stranger to the suit may not be considered in the suit." A procurator, since he acts for the person he represents by reason of his special mandate,[272] must not be excluded in this matter as a third person. He must rather be included among those who are capable of committing a prejudicial attempt.

In the chapter of the Code on the "Intervention of a Third Person in a Cause," canon 1852 permits intervention in any instance of a trial until the cause is concluded. The reason for allowing such intervention is that the trial may be more swiftly and easily expedited. The intervention after the closing of the cause (*conclusio in causa*), when it is permitted by the parties of the trial, will not be a prejudicial

[269] Canon 1854: "... altera pars adversus alteram aut ipse iudex adversus alterutram vel utramque partem...."

[270] *Elucubrationes Diversae,* Lib. II, tit. 16, *de attentatis,* n. 46.

[271] *A Practical Commentary on the Code of Canon Law* (2. ed., 2 vols., 1948, New York: Joseph F. Wagner, Inc.), II, 326.

[272] Canon 1659, § 1.—Procurator ne prius a iudice admittatur quam speciale mandatum ad lites scriptum, etiam in calce ipsius citationis, mandantis subscriptione munitum, et locum, diem, mensem et annum referens, apud tribunal deposuerit.

attempt. Hanssen[273] states that, if one of the parties dissents, the intervention after the closing of the cause would be a prejudicial atempt that is automatically void.

In the matter of appeals, the consequences of the appellant committing a prejudicial attempt must be noted. A decree of the Rota,[274] which cites Schmalzgrueber,[275] decided a cause presented to it as follows: if the appellant commits a prejudicial attempt, the effect of which is contrary to his appeal, he proves himself unworthy of the remedy against the sentence, which the appeal affords. The judge of the earlier judicial instance (*iudex a quo*) can then proceed against the appellant as though the appeal had not been made, since the sentence immediately becomes irrevocably adjudged.[276] This is so, since the appellant by his attempt in violation of the appeal tacitly renounces the appeal. Though canon 1740, § 2, mentions only an express renunciation made in writing, nevertheless the Code, just as pre-Code law, holds all prejudicial attempts in abhorrence. Thus, the principal cause is regularly suspended upon the occasion of a prejudicial attempt;[277] the judge must decree its revocation or purgation, once it is proved.[278]

[273] "De canctione nullitatis in processu canonico," *Apollinaris*, XI (1938), 401.

[274] S.R.R., *Decisiones*, XXIX (1937), p. 596, dec. LX, n. 3.

[275] *Ius Ecclesiasticum*, Lib. II, tit. 28, n. 123.

[276] S.R.R., *Decisiones, loc. cit.*: "Si vero pars appellans pendente appellatione attentet aliquid, considerandum, an id quod attentatur, sit immediate contrarium appellationi propriae, an vero non. Si primum, non revocatur, sed appellationis favore privatur appellans; quia dum propria auctoritate ius sibi dicit, iudicem appellationis contempsisse censetur; ideoque beneficio appellationis indignum se reddit; frustra enim invocat auxilium legis, qui committit in legem, quin et attentando aliquid contra primam appellationem, censetur eidem renuntiasse, eamque deseruisse. Quare hoc casu sententia, a qua appellatum est, statim transit in rem iudicatam, ita ut iudex a quo perinde, ac se appellatum non esset, ad executionem, possit procedere."

[277] Canon 1856, § 1.—Pendente quaestione de attentato, cursus causae principalis regulariter suspenditur....

[278] Canon 1857, § 1.—Demonstrato attentato, iudex decernere debet eius revocationem seu purgationem.

The Sacred Roman Rota considers an attempt committed by the appellant as a tacit renunciation. Therefore, the appellant loses his right to pursue the appeal.[279]

In an appeal the judge of the previous instance may be tempted to act when he no longer is competent, therein forgetting that an appeal *ipso facto* prolongs the pending of the litigation.[280] Once an appeal *in suspensivo* is interposed, the jurisdiction of the judge is suspended. Moreover, the sentence of the judge of the earlier instance cannot be put into execution. If an appeal has ben made according to the requirements of law, the sentence, even though valid, is suspended; no execution of the sentence can take place; the judge against whom the appeal proceeds is forbidden to act any further in the matter. Noval[281] states that the execution of the sentence is postponed until the cause on appeal is reviewed and the sentence of the prior judge receives confirmation or is ordered changed.

The entire process of reviewing the appeal made *in suspensivo* is protected from any further proceedings of the lower court in the matter appealed. If the judge of the lower court proceeds to act within the ten days allowed for an appeal, or after the notice of the appeal has been given,[282] he commits a prejudicial attempt. Therefore, the judge may not even proceed to execute a valid sentence, at least until the appeal *in suspensivo* is concluded.[283]

[279] S.R.R., *Decisiones,* XXIX (1937), p. 597, dec. LX, n. 5: "Unde sequitur quod, si situatio ob culpam attentatis in praeiudicium alterius partis perior facta est, et quidem irreparabiliter, causa principalis decerni nequit, seu appellans, si is fuerit attentans, decidit e iure appellationem prosequendi." Cf. Maranta, *Speculum Aureum,* Pars VI, n. 194.

[280] Canon 1889, § 1.—Appellatio in suspensivo exsecutionem appellatae sententiae suspendit ac propterea in suo robore permanet principium: 'lite pendente nihil innovetur.'... § 2. Omnis appellatio est in suspensivo, nisi aliud in iure expresse caveatur, firmo praescripto canon 1917, § 2...

[281] *De Iudiciis,* n. 653.

[282] Cf. canon 1882.

[283] The following illustrations, listed by Roberti in the *Apollinaris*

A definitive sentence is invalid if it is pronounced while an appeal is pending in the same cause from an interlocutory sentence which had a definitive force.[284] If the judge in the earlier judicial instance (*iudex a quo*) pronounces a definitive sentence in such an event, he commits a prejudicial attempt against the appellant.[285]

Schmalzgrueber[286] and Bouix[287] held that the judge of the previous instance could occasionally without incurring the *vitium attentati* act in a cause which had been appealed. The general rule was that the judge in the earlier judicial instance was permitted to do everything which would help the appeal and expedite the cause itself. Since canon 1854 must be understood along with canon 1889, the judge of the prior instance would still be permitted to put into effect the prescriptions of canons 1672 and 1673, if he foresees a party's interests will be prejudiced. Therefore he could sequestrate the litigious object or pronounce a temporary prohibition against the exercise of a particular right, if he foresees that the use of such a right will be injurious to the interests of the other litigant.

(VIII [1935], p. 40-42), will indicate some of the attempts of which a judge could be guilty: "*Attentatum* quod in pluribus causis habetur (c. 1854), e.g., si iudex primae vel secundae instantiae praesumat causam etiam in ulteriore instantia iudicare (cfr. c. 1594, § 1-4), si iudex secundae instantiae sibi arroget causas iudicatas a tribunalibus non sibi subiectis (cfr. c. 1594, § 1-4), si Rota praetendat iudicare de nullitate propriae sententiae (c. 1603, § 1, 3°) aut de restitutione in integrum contra illas (c. 1603, § 1, 4°), si iudices audeant definire nullitatem sententiarum quae non fuerint ab ipsis prolatae (c. 1893, 1895) aut contra easdem concedere ex rationibus facti restitutionem in integrum (c. 1905, § 2, 1°-3°) aut eandem restitutionem indulgere contra sententias a se prolatas sed ex rationibus iuris (c. 1905, § 2, 4°) aut iudicare de tertii oppositione quae ad ipsos non pertineat (c. 1899, § 1), aut tandem exsequi sententias extra casus a iure definitas (c. 1920, § 1-3). Idem dicendum si iudex praesumat iterum iudicare causam iam definitam sententia quae nequeat amplius impugnari."

[284] Cf. *supra*, page 105.

[285] S.R.R., *Decisiones*, XXX (1938), dec. LI, pp. 472-477.

[286] *Ius Ecclesiasticum*, Lib. II, tit. 28, nn. 115-118.

[287] *De Judiciis*, II, 288.

It must be remembered that an appeal pends from the moment that the sentence is pronounced by the judge. If the appeal itself has not been interposed, the pending of the appeal, nevertheless, takes place immediately. Once the sentence is made known to the litigants, the period of ten days granted by the Code[288] to make an appeal becomes effective. During this period the judge cannot put the sentence into execution. This is so, even though no appeal has been interposed.[289] The appeal continues to pend after it has been interposed before the judge of the earlier judicial instance (*iudex a quo*).[290] Roberti[291] makes the observation that the principles of canon 1854 regarding prejudicial attempts committed during the pending litigation are applicable also to attempts undertaken during a pending appeal. This conclusion is shown by the use of the expressions *"intra decem dies"* of canon 1881 and *"inter mensem"* of canon 1883, since canon 1854 includes as attempts the violations of the terms assigned by law or by the judge to the parties for the placing of judicial acts.[292]

Thus, by the clear statement in canon 1854 of who is capable of committing a prejudicial attempt, it is seen how the legislator wishes to insure the meting out of justice against any attempt of the parties and to protect the litigants against the arbitrariness of the judge. There should be no question, therefore, as to who the perpetrator of a prejudicial attempt actually is, since the canon excludes all others connected with the judicial proceedings except the plaintiff, the defendant or the judge.

[288] Canon 1881.

[289] Canon 1917, § 1.—Sententia quae transiit in rem iudicatam executioni mandari potest. Three means whereby a matter becomes irrevocably adjudbed are set forth in canon 1902. Cf. Roberti, *De Processibus*, II, n. 476; Lega, *De Iudiciis*, I, n. 625.

[290] Cf. canons 1882-1883; 1725; 1889.

[291] *Op. Cit.*, II, n. 476.

[292] Canon 1854: "... sive respiciat terminos partibus a iure vel a iudice assignatos ad ponendos certos actus iudiciales."

ARTICLE 3. THE INNOVATION AS A TRUE CHANGE OF THE JUDICIAL SITUATION

The innovation or prejudiical attempt[293] that is null *ipso iure* by reason of canon 1855, § 1, must reflect a real change. This change must affect the object or the nature of the litigation or the judicial terms. Therefore, any attempt that is merely apparent would not be an innovation according to the meaning conveyed by canon 1854. An act of pure administration,[294] which does not change the state of possession at the beginning of a trial—such as measures directed to the maintenance of property—does not constitute a prejudicial attempt. Likewise, a second marriage contracted while the first is under litigation is not automatically (*per se*) invalid; if the first marriage is tuly invalid, the second marriage will be valid, as far as reference to the pending litigation is concerned.

The Code (canon 1854) in what it postulates for prejudicial attempts leaves possible room for two kinds of innovations: those which concern the matter or object under litigation, and those which concern time-limits (*termini*) which are determined by law, by the judge, or by the agreement of the parties.[295]

SECTION A. INNOVATIONS CONCERNING THE MATTER UNDER LITIGATION[296]

Wernz-Vidal indicated the following division in the in-

[293] Cf. canon 1854.

[294] Coronata, *Institutiones*, III, n. 1416: "Nota tamen non esse considerandum ut *attentatum* actum iudicis continuativum iuris aut possessionis."

[295] Canon 1634, § 2.—Termini autem iudiciales et conventionales, ante eorum lapsum, poterunt, iusta intercedente causa, a iudice, auditis vel petentibus partibus, prorogari.

[296] Cf. Wernz-Vidal, *Ius Canonicum*, VI, nn. 570 ff.; Lega-Bartoccetti, *Commentarius*, II, 894 ff.; Roberti, *De Processibus*, II, n. 431; Vermeersch-Creusen, *Epitome Iuris Canonici*, III, 105; Noval, *De Iudiciis*, n. 602; Coronata, *Institutiones*, III, n. 1385; Cappello, *Summa Iuris Canonici*, III, 248; Regatillo, *Institutiones*, II, 241; Blat, *De Processibus*, Lib. IV, p. 361.

novations that are directed to the litigious matter: (1) those which affect the remote matter, i.e., the litigious matter itself, or a right which is controverted, and (2) those which affect the proximate matter, i.e., the suit or its judicial instance.[297]

The following are examples of prejudicial attempts committed against the litigious matter: (1) alienating or selling the object of controversy during the pending litigation; (2) separating a married couple, or denying them their marital rights, while a cause is pending by reason of some alleged diriment impediment;[298] (3) proceeding to a new election, postulation, nomination or conferral of a benefice with prejudice to either litigant; (4) transferring the ownership of a litigious object or right.

These attempts or any others that change the litigious matter are usually extrajudicial acts. While such prejudicial attempts are null *ipso iure,* they do not render the judicial process itself invalid, since there is no causal connection between them and the procedural acts.[299]

[297] *Op. cit.*, VI, n. 572: "Ex notione data attentati patet hoc referri posse: 1) ad litis materiam, sub quo nomine venit a) res ipsa litigiosa vel ius controversum, quae sunt iudicii materia remota; b) *actiones* ipsae seu intantiae iudiciales, quae litis materia proxima sunt." Cf. Noval, *op. cit.*, n. 602; Coronata, *op. cit.*, III, n. 1385; Goyeneche, *De Processibus*, I, pt. 2, n. 95; Blat, *op. cit.*, p. 361: "... innovatio *respiciat litis materiam* quoad ius, possessionem, etiam precariam. . . ." Augustine (*A Commentary*, VII, 298) stated that the judicial action or suit may be such that it relates either to persons or to things.

[298] They are to be separated if they are still living together and grave scandal exists. Cf. S.C. de Sacramentis, instr., *Provida Mater*, 15 aug. 1936; Art. 63—*AAS*, XXVIII (1936), 327; Art. 223—*AAS*, XXVIII (1936), 357. See also Doheny, *Canonical Procedure in Matrimonial Cases* (2. ed., 2 vols., The Bruce Publishing Co., Milwaukee, 1948), I, 205 (hereafter cited as *Canonical Procedure*) and Torre, *Processus Matrimonialis* (3. ed., Neapoli, 1956), p. 200.

[299] Hanssen, "De sanctione nullitatis in processu canonico," *Apollinaris*, XI (1938), p. 402, n. 92: "Illa [innovatio circa materiam] fit actibus extraiudicialibus durante processu circa litis obiectum positis; ipsum processum non reddit invalidum." Cf. Wernz-Vidal, *Ius Canonicum*, VI, n. 572; Roberti, *De Processibus*, II, n. 431. If the attempt

Within the classification of innovations affecting the matter or the object of litigation are to be included all substantial transgressions of procedural law, provided, of course, that they are prejudicial to the other party. This may be seen from the following. Canon 1731 treats of any change made in the bill of complaint (*libellus*) after the joinder of issue has taken place. Canon 1731, 1°, decrees: The plaintiff is not permitted to change the bill of complaint unless, with the consent of the defendant, the judge considers for a just reason that the change should be admitted. Furthermore, the defendant always has a right to compensation for damages and expenses, if they are due to him. The bill of complaint is not considered changed, if the method of proof is shortened or altered; if the petition to the court or some accessory petition be lessened; if circumstances of a fact already mentioned in the bill of complaint are illustrated, completed or amended, so that the object of controversy remains the same; if, in place of the object of litigation, the price, interest or something equivalent is asked.

Coronata[300] discusses, in connection with the change made in the bill of complaint, the difference between *mutatio libelli* and *emendatio libelli.* The first evinces any substantial change that is made; the latter reflects any change that is purely accidental. Before the joinder of issue takes place, the plaintiff can make substantial as well as accidental changes in the bill of complaint. This is clear from the wording of canon 1731.[301] Any substantial change in the bill of complaint, if it is made without the permission of the defendant after the joinder of issue, is a prejudicial attempt. This is so, since the purpose of the plaintiff, that is, the object of the trial as stated in the bill of complaint, is determined by the joinder of issue.[302]

is a procedural act, all the acts which follow it and depend upon it will be null and void (cf. canon 1680, § 2).

300 *Institutiones*, III, n. 1256.

301 "Lite contestata: 1° Haud licet actori libellum mutare. . . ."

302 Canon 1726; Hanssen, *ibid.*, p. 397: "Lite contestata non licet

In general, any change that affects the litigious object of a pending lawsuit is to be considered a prejudicial attempt. The Code does make an exception to this general rule, however.[303] The reason for this exception is that the absolute maintenance of the *status quo* during the judicial process might cause inconvenience by favoring the machinations of an unscrupulous party. If changes in regard to the litigious object were ruled out entirely, then the way might be paved for an injurious change to ensue from the very observance of canon 1854 itself. Therefore the Code will authorize a certain surety, called sequestration. Thus canon 1854 will permit the judge to invoke canons 1672, 1673, in order to sequestrate the object of controversy, to interdict the use of a right, or to order the sequestration of a debtor's possessions, all of which by analogy can serve as sureties.

SECTION B. INNOVATIONS CONCERNING THE JUDICIAL TERMS

The canons[304] which govern the judicial terms are to be found under the heading of the Code, *"De dilationum terminis et fatalibus."* A *dilatio* denotes a warranted interval of time granted to the parties for the placing of some procedural act, whereas a *terminus* points to the final moment of this interval.[305] Though the two words are often used interchangeably, a *dilatio* is the time within which an act must be placed; the *terminus* is the day or the hour at which the act must already have been placed. These terms or intervals

actori libellum mutare nisi reus consentiat et iudex iustis de causis censeat mutationem esse admittendum (c. 1731, n. 1°). De iustis causis iudicat iudex, sed nisi reus consentiat mutatio libelli est attentatum, quod est ipso iure nullum (c. 1854, 1855)." Regatillo (*Institutiones*, II, p. 241, n. 630) states that accidental corrections in the bill of complaint after the joinder of issue are not attempts.

303 Canon 1854: "... sive innovatio respiciat litis materiam, salvo tamen praescripto canon 1672, 1673. . . ."

304 Canons 1634-1635.

305 Cf. Wernz-Vidal, *Ius Canonicum*, VI, n. 181; Roberti, *De Processibus*, I, n. 180 (4. ed.).

are provided for in the law, since justice must be protected. They are granted to the parties for the obtaining of counsel, for the producing of new witnesses or documents, or for the performing of certain acts prescribed or provided for (e.g., appeal) by law. Then, again, they may be employed for a shortening of the trial, since the negligence of parties and the inactivity of the judges could at times draw out the trial indefinitely. Consequently there would arise a detriment to the public or private good. The terms are binding upon all who participate in the judicial process, even the promoter of justice and the defender of the bond.[306]

The judicial terms or limits for action can be divided into three categories, in line with the authority from which they derive, in line with the effect which they produce, or with reference to the stage in a process at which they occur.[307] However, it is the first category that is the more important in a discussion of prejudicial attempts. If the terms are established by law, by the judge or by the litigants with judicial approval, they are called respectively legal,[308] judicial or conventional terms. In regard to the last (conventional terms), the parties were formerly permitted to agree upon certain terms. Now, however, this freedom is curtailed by the requirement of canon 1634, § 2, that the judge approve the prolongation of conventional terms; their juridic force will depend upon the approval given by the judge.[309]

The following terms are prescribed by the law itself: ten days for the seeking of redress against the rejection of

[306] Cf. canons 1987 and 1996.

[307] Cf. Wernz-Vidal, *Ius Canonicum*, VI, n. 182; Roberti, *De Processibus* (4. ed.), I, n. 180.

[308] Legal terms are called *fatalia legis* or simply *fatalia*. The *fatalia legis* are the terms which the law establishes so firmly that the judge cannot extend them. These *fatalia* are established by law for the purpose of an ultimate termination of the continued use of rights. Cf. Coronata, *Institutiones*, III, n. 1157; Lega-Bartoccetti, *Commentarius*, I, p. 265, n. 2, and p. 268, n. 6.

[309] Roberti, *De Processibus* (4. ed.), I, n. 181.

the bill of complaint (can. 1709, § 3); for the prosecution of a cause, two years in the first instance and one year in the second instance with the consequent result of abatement (can. 1736); two months for his demonstration of right by the one who has announced the launching of a new enterprise (can. 1676, § 3); three days to reject witnesses (can. 1764, § 4); three months for seeking a *restitutio in integrum* in the event of contempt of court (can. 1847); a week after the first discussion of the judges for the pronouncing of the sentence (can. 1871, § 5); two years in first instance and one year thereafter for the concluding of the instance (can. 1620); ten days for the lodging of an appeal (can. 1881); a month for the prosecuting of the appeal (can. 1883); three months for lodging a complaint of remediable nullity (can. 1895); thirty years for lodging a complaint of irremediable nullity (can. 1893); four years for seeking a warranted erstwhile status (*restitutio in integrum* [can. 1688; 1905, § 1]); four months for the executing of the sentence (can. 1922, § 2).[310]

The judge determines all the terms which are not designated or fixed by the law itself. Thus, he assigns a term for: the citation (can. 1714; 1720, § 2); the defendant's appearance in court (can. 1712); the joinder of issue (can. 1728); the removal of the charge of contempt of court (can. 1729, § 1); the production of proofs (can. 1731, 2°; 1860, 2°); the petition for an interrogation of witnesses (can. 1761, § 2); the presentation of any warranted defense (can. 1862, § 1).[311]

In general, legal terms (*fatalia legis*) cannot be extended by the judge, if these terms are absolutely determined by the law.[312] These terms are so constituted that upon the lapse of the indicated term the right under application is lost and the judge is not empowered to revive it. Neverthe-

[310] Cf. Wernz-Vidal, *Ius Canonicum,* VI, n. 185; Roberti, *op. cit.,* I, n. 181.

[311] Cf. Wernz-Vidal, *loc. cit.,* Roberti, *loc. cit.*

[312] Cf. canons 1790, § 3; 1610, § 3; 1881; 1736; 1847; 1895; 1893; 1905, § 1.

less if the terms, though they were established by law, require the intervention of the judge,[313] he may extend them before they have lapsed.[314] In some cases the law will extend the term. Canon 1885 grants to heirs and successors, in line with the ruling stated in canon 1733, an extension of the term for an appeal.

Judicial and conventional terms may be extended by the judge either at the request of the parties or also *ex officio*.[315] A just cause on the part of the litigants is any real need of a longer period of time for the performance of the act in behalf of which the respite is granted, e.g., preparation of proof in a difficult cause. The public good which is inextricably bound up with the controversy may require an extension of time through an approval from the judge. The promoter of justice in marriage causes is not excluded by the law from petitioning for an extension of time.[316]

During the extended interval of time, the judge is forbidden to take further judicial action in regard to the cause, or the article of the cause, for which the added interval was granted. Accordingly, acts placed by him in violation of the terms are null as prejudicial attempts. The judge is not forbidden, however, to proceed further in whatever acts of a cause are for their performance not confined within the established interval itself.[317] Moreover, the judicial

[313] Cf. canons 1764, § 4; 1883; 1676, § 3. It is to be noted that, though the term of four months for the execution of the sentence in personal suits (can. 1922, § 3) is not peremptory, it may be extended six months or shortened to two.

[314] Roberti, *De Processibus*, I, n. 180: "Lapsus termini dicitur momentum quo terminus seu dilatio exspirat."

[315] Wernz-Vidal, *Ius Canonicum*, VI, n. 185: "Termini iudiciales et conventionales possunt a iudice prorogari sive ad instantiam partium sive propria auctoritate, auditis partibus, dummodo iusta intercedat causa et prorogatio fiat ante lapsum termini. . . ."

[316] Wernz-Vidal, *op. cit.*, VI, n. 185.

[317] Wernz-Vidal, *op. cit.*, VI, n. 187: "Iudicis officium toto dilationis tempore conquiescit sive quoad totam causam sive quoad specialem actum causae, propter quem dilatio fuit concessa. Quare si iudex

acts for which a peremptory term was granted, as long as they are undertaken after the lapse of the term, are null. The reason is that a right has been acquired by the other party against a new term.[318]

In conclusion, the conditions for a prejudicial attempt in violation of the judicial terms can be stated as follows: 1. The act must be placed by one of the litigants or by the judge, the while the other party or both parties dissent; 2. the act must be prejudicial to the party or parties; 3. the act must be either: a) the prolongation or shortening of a term by the judge;[319] b) the placing of a judicial act contrary to the cause or article of the cause during the term granted; c) the executing of a judiical act outside the allotted time when a term for its performance was assigned, or d) the granting of a new term after a peremptory term has lapsed.[320] Thus, prejudicial attempts committed against the terms assigned by the judge or by the law to the parties for the placing of certain judicial acts[321] not only are null

nondum elapso dilationis tempore ad ulteriora procedit, nulla et irrita sunt acta iudicialia; sed minime prohibetur, quominus in iis actibus causae procedat, pro quibus dilatio non fuit concessa."

[318] Roberti, *De Processibus*, I (4. ed.), n. 185: "Actus positi elapso termino peremptorio sunt nulli; quia ius iam acquisitum est alteri parti. In hoc casu arbitraria concessio novi termini, itemque arbitraria coarctatio constituere possunt attentatum. . . ."

[319] S.R.R., *Decisiones*, XXX (1938), dec. LI, p. 475, n. 5: "Casus autem in can. 1854 relati demonstrative referuntur, quoniam quaelibet perversio ordinis processualis in praeiudicium partium facta potest attentatum constituere." Cf. Roberti, *De Processibus*, II, n. 154; Ciprotti, "De novis probationibus post conclusionem in causa," *Apollinaris*, XII (1939), p. 111; Hanssen, "De sanctione nullitatis in processu canonico," *Apollinaris*, XI (1938), p. 402.

[320] Cf. Wernz-Vidal, *Ius Canonicum*, VI, n. 574: "Quare ut adsit in hac parte attentatum, haec requiruntur: 1°) Ut actus positus fuerit extra terminos concessos, vel ut intra terminos actus ponatur qui sit contrarius iuri partibus competenti ex dilatione et terminorum praefixione. . . ." Cf. also Coronata, *Institutiones*, III, n. 1385; Roberti, *De Processibus*, II, n. 431.

[321] Canon 1854: ". . . terminos partibus a iure vel a iudice assignatos ad ponendos certos actus iudiciales."

ipso iure[322] but also may void other acts which depend upon them.[323]

Ciprotti, in speaking of the nullity of proof admitted by the judge after conclusion of the cause[324] without having heard the other party, concluded: if the nullity results by reason of canon 1861, § 2 (*"aliter iudicium nullius est momenti"*), it is clear that such nullity affects not only the acts done contrary to this canon, but also the whole process and even the sentence, whether it depends on or abstracts from such invalid proof. On the contrary, if the nullity results solely from the attempt against the term, then solely the attempt is null by reason of canon 1855, § 1; but the nullity of the process and of the sentence will follow if they are entailed through the rule stated in canon 1680, § 2 (*"nullitas alicuius actus ... importat nullitatem actorum qui ... subsequuntur et ab actu ... dependent."*). The remedy against such nullity will be either a suit for obtaining a declaration of nullity according to canon 1855, or the plaint of nullity against the sentence itself.[325]

322 Canon 1855, § 1.

323 Canon 1680, § 2.—Nullitas alicius actus non importat nullitatem actorum qui praecedunt aut subsequuntur et ab actu non dependent.

324 Cf. canons 1860-1862.

325 "De novis probationibus post conclusionem in causa," *Apollinaris*, XII (1939), 111: "... si quis adhuc dubitet de vera can. 1861, § 2 ... significatione, quodlibet dubium auferri potest ex aliis Codicis normis. Iudex enim qui ita se gerat ..., attentatum committit, quia lite pendente aliquid in praeiudicium partis innovat, sine eius consensu; nam casus attentatorum in can. 1854 relati sunt non taxative sed mere demonstrative.... Atqui *attentata sunt ipso iure nulla* (c. 1855, § 1), ita ut etiam ex hoc capite nullitas in casu habeatur.

"Interest tamen utrum nullitas habeatur etiam ex ipso can. 1861, § 2, sicut nos censemus, an vero solum ex can. 1855, § 1, seu ex attentato. Num si nullitas est ex ipso can. 1861, § 2, cum inibi sanctio ita statuatur: *aliter iudicium nullius est momenti* ..., patet nullitate affici non solum actus qui fit contra praescriptum can. 1861, § 2, id est probatio quae inaudita parte admittatur, sed totus processus et sententia, sive ab illa probatione dependeat sive non. E contra, si nullitas solum ex attentato habeatur, ipsum attentatum est utique nullum, ad

A final observation is now in place in regard to the judicial order and attempts. It can be stated as a rule that a prejudicial attempt obtains every time the judicial order suffers an inversion that is injurious to one or both of the parties. Wernz-Vidal observe, however, that such an inversion could be an act of negligence in fulfillment of the office, which is governed by canon 1625. Therefore, if it is actually a question of negligence on the part of the judge, it will not give rise to an incidental question on attempts. He will, nevertheless, be bound to indemnify the damages inflicted upon the parties of the trial.[326]

ARTICLE 4. INNOVATION AGAINST THE WILL OF THE PARTY

The requirement for a prejudicial attempt that the innovation militate against the will of the party concerned is probably more important than all the others which are set down in canon 1854. It is also more easily understood than the others, since there can be no prejudicial attempt as such, if the consent of the party or parties is given to the innovation. Therefore, though all the other requirements are present, as long as the innovation is not placed against the

normam can. 1855, § 1, sed iudicii et sententiae nullitas non habeatur nisi secundum can. 1680, § 2, statuentem: *nullitas alicuius actus ... importat nullitatem actorum qui ... subsequuntur et ab actu dependent;* ita ut si, e.g., iudex in sententiam omnino reiciat probationem, vel si ex probatione admissa nulla notitia haberi possit quae ad causam pertineat, iuxta hanc alteram opinionem iudicium valet. Remedium autem contra huiusmodi nullitatem est vel recursus ad normam can. 1855, vel etiam querela nullitatis contra sententiam." Roberti, "Circa limites querelae nullitatis et restitutionis in integrum," *Apollinaris,* I (1928), 477-478: "... a) Quoad nullitates iuris positivi, recolimus praecipuas rationes ob quas Codex comminatur actuum nullitatem: ... 6) Si commissa fuerint attentata ... et sententia iisdem innitatur (c. 1682, § 2)."

326 *Ius Canonicum,* VI, n. 574: "Attentatum relate ad treminos partibus concessos ... committitur, cum actus intra terminum praefixum non ponitur ... quodsi agitur de ipso iudice, poterit esse actus negligentiae in officio implendo, qui ipsum obliget ad indemnitatem praestandam pro damnis inde partibus inlatis (can. 1625)."

will of the interested party there is no prejudicial attempt.

With the consent of the party, no one is attacked or harmed. Instead of an injurious act, a form of *transactio* or settlement[327] takes place, by which the object or the nature of the action in progress is modified. That such a settlement should take place is readily seen, since canon 1925 declares it desirable and fully within the limits of the law. The agreement entered into by those concerned may terminate the principal cause as well as the incidental cause concerning which there would otherwise be an attempt. The settlement, however, is supposedly restricted here to an incidental matter which would arise, and the party in question has consented; here there is an accord. Whether or not the agreement terminates the principal cause will depend upon the intention of the parties. This may be illustrated as follows: ordinarily the alienation of a possession according to canon 1854 will constitute a prejudicial attempt. It is not inconceivable, however, that the possessor might be willing to give the matter in question to the other party, pending the outcome of the trial. If he does so, there will be no question of a prejudicial attempt.

There is, however, some question regarding the terminology employed by the authors in their discussion of the requirement that the party dissent. Such phrases as "*cum dissensu,*" "*parte dissentiente,*" and "*dissensus*" are used for the most part. Nevertheless, Wernz-Vidal[328] remark that the act of innovation must necessarily be undertaken "*citra consensum*" of the party, or they require that the party be "*dissentiens.*" Roberti[329] uses the terms "*sine consenu*" and "*dissentiens.*" Obviously these authors are employing the terms as being equivalent. It must be observed, however, that a real distinction can be made between "*parte dissentiente,*" as employed by the Code, and "*sine consensu,*" which

[327] Cf. canon 1925.

[328] *Ius Canonicum,* VI, n. 574.

[329] *De Processibus,* II, n. 430.

distinction would destroy the effectiveness of the latter term so far as prejudicial attempts are concerned.

A person who dissents is one who makes a positive act of the will against something, whereas a person who is considered as being without consent may be totally passive, not having expressed any positive will either for or against anything. Thus, in the use of the phrase *"sine consensu,"* a doubt remains regarding what the person really willed, if indeed he expressed any positive will at all. Conceivably a person could be ignorant of the executed prejudicial act undertaken against him. Then he will indeed be without consent, but he still could be a person not dissenting. This is so, since he has no knowledge of the act upon which his own will-act must be based: *"nihil volitum, nisi cognitum."* Such a person neither dissents nor consents, but is rather without consent.

Dissent is the antonym of consent. Once, however, the preposition "without" is used with "consent," the completed phrase is not necessarily synoymous with dissent. Therefore, to avoid any ambiguity, the term "dissent" should always be used in preference to "without consent." It seems as a consequence that there must be dissent, by way of a positive act, before there can exist any prejudicial attempt. This position, however, appears rather severe. One should rather take the view of Coronata, who regards as interchangeable the two elements of dissent and prejudice as expressed in the phrase *"parte dissentiente et in eius praeiudicium,"* so that the nullity of the attempt can arise from the presence of either of these elements.[330] He then concludes that dissent is presumed if the injured party is not aware of the prejudicial act. If, on the other hand, the party does have knowledge of the attempt, his dissent will not be presumed, since "he who is silent appears to consent,"[331] provided of course that the party had the opportunity of uttering his dissent.

[330] *Institutiones,* III, n. 1386.

[331] Reg. 43, R.J., in VI°: "Qui tacet consentire videtur." Cf. Bar-

Article 5. Innovation as Prejudicial to the Party

The concepts of prejudice and dissent are very closely related in the consideration of prejudicial attempts. This fact is evidenced by the wording of the Code,[332] "*parte dissentiente et in eius praeiudicium.*" Dissent, or at least the lack of consent, as noted at the conclusion of the foregoing article, and prejudice must both be verified. Prejudice must be understood here as the damage resulting from an act placed contrary to the party's procedural intentions in the suit. A prejudicial attempt, therefore, is committed only when it is to the detriment of others.[333] Such detriment, injury or prejudice will not come about if there is consent to the action in question on the part of the interested party.[334]

There are, nevertheless, certain situations wherein the innovation will not be prejudicial to the party, even though he dissents. In such events he will be considered as one who is unreasonably unwilling if he does dissent. The Code (can. 1854) leaves room for two exceptions to the general rule, namely, with reference to sequestration and the prohibition to exercise a right.[335] Though sequestration is advantageous to the party not in possession, the possessor is without any real complaint. No injury is done to the possessor, since sequestration has for its purpose the prevention of any injury or violation of the law, which would or

toccetti, *De Regulis Iuris Canonici* (Romae: Angelo Belardetti Editore —1955), p. 165.

332 Canon 1854.

333 D. (4. 17) 74: "Non debet alteri per alterum iniqua condicio inferri." Cf. Roberti, *De Processibus*, II, n. 430; Noval, *De Iudiciis*, n. 630.

334 In canon 1800, § 4, "*praeiudicium*" is used in its literal meaning of a "prejudgment," since a *praesumptio iuris* arises from the refusal of a party apart from a legitimate cause to submit to the court a sample of his writing. However, in the other canons of the Code, "*praeiudicium*" is used in the transferred sense of damage, harm or injury. Cf. canons 800; 779; 1623, § 1; 435, § 3; 1312, §2; 1654, § 1; 1899, § 3; etc.

335 Cf. canons 1672-1673.

at least could ensue if the object of litigation were lost or diminished in any way.

Another example of an innovation which would not be prejudicial is the following. If a party has in his possession an immovable object whose ownership is being contested, and makes repairs on it (even more than simple maintenance repairs), he does not commit a prejudicial attempt. The reason is that he inflicts no damage on his adversary, who might later be declared the owner of the object under litigation. Its value has rather been enhanced by the repairs. Marchesi suggests other possible exceptions to the rule, such as the necessity for food.[336]

[336] *Summula Iuris Canonici,* II, 179: "Ergo non licet alienatio rei controversae nisi ex causa necessaria, puta alimentorum, aut pro solutione funeris, vel ex causa iusta a iudice approbata, v.g., si res alias perirent. . . ."

CHAPTER V

NULLITY OF PREJUDICIAL ATTEMPTS AND THE ACTION GRANTED AGAINST THEM

ARTICLE 1. THE NULLITY OF PREJUDICIAL ATTEMPTS[1]

Canon 1855, § 1, states: "Attempts are null *ipso iure*."[2] The provision of the Code is the basis for the action granted against prejudicial attempts.[3] In the previous chapter, the various requirements for a prejudicial attempt were set down as contained in canon 1854. These same requirements were more particularly determined therein, especially that of the pending of the litigation. Therefore it is unnecessary to comment upon them further, except in so far as there is need to single out a particular bearing they may have on the nullity of an attempt.

At this point the Code settled an uncertainty that existed in the pre-Code law on whether attempts were null *ipso iure* or simply rescissible.[4] No longer, however, can there be any doubt that a prejudicial attempt is automatically null, provided all the postulated conditions of canon 1854

[1] Cf. Roberti, *De Processibus*, II, n. 432; Noval, *De Iudiciis*, n. 604; Goyeneche, *De Processibus*, I, pt. 2, p. 131; Coronata, *Institutiones*, III, n. 1386.

[2] "Attentata sunt ipso iure nulla." Cf. Reg. 64, R.J., in VI°: "Quae contra ius fiunt, debent utique pro infectis haberi." Cf. also Bartoccetti, *De Regulis Iuris Canonici*, p. 217: "Citari ... recte poterat regula in pluribus locis Codicis in quibus irritantur acta ob non servatas aliquas substantiales normas legis...." and Roberti, *loc. cit.*

[3] Cf. canons 1855, §§ 2-3; 1856-1857.

[4] Cf. Roberti, *Codicis Iuris Canonici Schemata*, Lib. IV, *De Processibus* (Romae: Typis Polyglottis Vaticanis, 1940), E, Can. 400, § 1, nota 3; Wernz, *Ius Decretalium*, V, n. 697; Schmalzgrueber, *Ius Ecclesiasticum*, Lib. II, tit. 28, nn. 122 ff.; Lega, *De Iudiciis*, I, n. 581; Reiffenstuel, *Ius Canonicum*, Lib. II, tit. 16, n. 35; Bouix, *De Judiciis*, 285 ff.

are present. It has already been discussed[5] how closely allied are the requirements that there be dissent, or at least the lack of consent, and that the act be prejudicial to the respective party. Therefore, even though the innovation is placed by the other party or by the judge during the pending litigation and in volation of the litigious object or judicial terms, there will be no attempt null *ipso iure* if these requirements are not fulfilled.

ARTICLE 2. THE JUDICIAL ACTION AGAINST PREJUDICIAL ATTEMPTS

"Every right is protected by an action, unless it has been expressly decreed otherwise."[6] This statement of the Code is the basis for the second paragraph of canon 1855:[7] a judicial action avails for the injured party to obtain the declaration of nullity of the prejudicial attempt. A judicial action was classically defined by Justinian in his *Institutiones*[8] as the "right of pursing in court what is due to oneself."

Though considerable discussion could attend one's study of the natures of a judicial action and of a right, to see if they are to be essentially differentiated, it will suffice here to set down what appears to be the preferred opinion. Coronata[9] holds that a judicial action is the public protection of a judicial right granted by positive law: the one differing from the other as the defender from that which is defended. Thus it seems preferable to hold that a real distinction does exist between the two, inasmuch as a judicial action does not always correspond to an objective right,

[5] Cf. *supra*, pages 123-125.

[6] Canon 1667: "Quodlibet ius . . . actione munitur, nisi aliud expresse cautum sit. . . ."

[7] § 2. "Idcirco parti ex attentato laesae competi actio ad obtiendam declarationem nullitatis."

[8] Inst. (4. 6): ". . . ius persequendi iudicio, quod sibi debetur." Cf. Roberti, *De Processibus* (4. ed.), I, n. 27; Wernz-Vidal, *Ius Canonicum*, VI, n. 244; Lega-Bartoccetti, *Commentarius*, I, p. 3, n. 5; Coronata, *Institutiones*, III, n. 1192.

[9] *Institutiones*, III, n. 1192, and p. 114, note 2.

nor does every objective right allow for the use of a corresponding judicial action in every event.[10]

Generally, a judicial action supposes objective and subjective elements. The objective elements are: (1) a law which makes a distribution of goods and rights among men; (2) an object which is the good or the right that is distributed (e.g., judicial protection); (3) a cause or a juridic fact which provides the reason for or title to such protection. Once the objective conditions for a judicial action are present, then subjective rights arise with their concomitant potential claims. The subjective elements are: (1) a subject who as a person possesses the right of judicial action; (2) the right itself for such action; (3) the interest or the usefulness which one obtains from judicial protection.[11] Though the Code does not expressly require this interest (*interesse*), a person will hardly trouble hmiself to press a suit in court unless he has something to gain thereby.[12]

The action granted by the Code[13] to the party injured by a prejudicial attempt is an action to obtain the declaration of nullity.[14]

In order to have a right to this action for the declaration of nullity, it is necessary that the act be *ipso iure* null. Canon 1680 states: the nullity of an act results only if it

[10] Cf. Roberti, *De Processibus* (4. ed.), I, nn. 28-30, 240; Lega-Bartoccetti, *Commentarius*, I, p. 356, nn. 4-5. Wernz-Vidal (*Ius Canonicum*, VI, n. 245), on the contrary, hold that no judicial action is granted without a corresponding right, and that no judicial action is to be denied its coherent right.

[11] Cf. Roberti, *De Processibus* (4. ed.), I, nn. 245-251, for a detailed discussion of these elements and conditions. See also Wernz-Vidal, *Ius Canonicum*, VI, n. 248; Coronata, *Institutiones*, III, n. 1192.

[12] Cf. Wernz-Vidal, *loc. cit.* Roberti (*op. cit.*, I, n. 251) notes that the Code indicates this element, though incidentally, when there is question of an action for nullity (can. 1679) or an occasion for intervention (can. 1852, § 1).

[13] Canon 1855, § 2.

[14] Canon 1679.—"Si actus aut contractus sit ipso iure nullus, datur ei, cuius interest, actio ad obtinendam a iudice declarationem nullitatis."

lacks the essential constituents of an act, or if it lacks certain formalities or conditions which under pain of nullity are required by the sacred canons. The nullity of any given act does not imply the nullity of other acts which precede or follow if they do not depend upon the act in question. Since the law prescribes, however, that an act be placed according to a certain form, will that act be null if the prescription of the law is not observed? In so far as this question bears on the matter of prejudicial attempts, the following principles can be stated. An act valid by the natural law, though prohibited by the positive law, is also valid according to the positive law, unless there is an express prohibition under pain of nullity. Such a prohibition is provided in canons 1854-1855, 1889. Accordingly, the canons of the Code[15] which prescribe judicial acts are expressly such that they involve the respective procedure in nullity unless the acts along with their prescribed forms are observed in accord with canon 1680. Thus, the prejudicial attempts mentioned in canon 1854 are, according to canon 1855, § 1, null *ipso iure* just as the acts of a process are null and void unless the promoter of justice or the defender of the bond is present as prescribed by the law in certain cases.[16]

Roberti[17] expresses a very important thought in regard to the nullity of an act, which is applicable also to prejudicial attempts. He states: the nullity of an act must be declared by the judge, otherwise the lapse of time or the tacit consent of the interested party will frequently sanate it. Such a sanation, however, does not result if the public good is involved, unless the law itself will grant a sanation for a greater public good.[18] Consequently, the injured party who

[15]Cf. canons 103; 150; 185; 542, 1°; etc. These especially are to be noted in regard to the nullity of procedural acts: canons 1558 and 1576 with can. 1892; 1585; 1587; 1659 with can. 1892; 1723; 1740; 1855; 1861; 1894.

[16] Cf. Roberti, *De Processibus*, I, n. 269; Lega-Bartoccetti, *Commentarius*, I, p. 411, n. 3; Coronata, *Institutiones*, III, n. 1210.

[17] *Op. Cit.*, I, n. 269 (IV).

[18] Cf. canons 1133, § 1; 1894, 1°-4°.

is aware of the prejudicial attempt must petition the judge to declare the attempt null;[19] otherwise, if the party acquiesces in the attempt, it will be sanated.[20]

Dissent of the party is presumed only when he has no knowledge of the prejudicial innovation. If the party is aware of the innovation and does not dissent, though he has the opportunity to do so, there is no prejudicial attempt. If after he knows of the attempt he still remains silent until the definitive sentence, then it can be looked upon either as an innovation which was placed with the consent of the party, or as an attempt which was sanated by his silence.[21]

According to the view of Roberti, the sanation of a null act obtains when the act is healed by the silence of the parties or by the passing of time. Generally, the nullity of acts involving merely a private interest is sanated through an express or tacit renunciation by the parties, whereas the nullity of public acts is sanated rather by the passing of time. Tacit approval is commonly presumed if the party has taken no action in regard to the nullity within ten days, or has willingly executed the null act, or has freely proceeded with the cause.[22]

It is evident that in a cause involving merely some private interest the party must petition the judge to declare the nullity of the attempt.[23] The interested party is not con-

[19] Cf. can. 1682, and Lega-Bartoccetti, *Commentarius*, II, p. 895, n. 5: "... Adeo ut videatur, declarationem nullitatis semper *ex officio* esse petendam. Etenim est ius lege quaesitum parti laesae quae tamen iuri suo de bonis privatis renunciare valet."

[20] Cf. Roberti, *op. cit.*, I, n. 269 (IV, 4); Goyeneche, *De Processibus*, I, pt. 2, p. 132: "Videntur ergo tales nullitates sanabiles." Coronata, *Institutiones*, III, n. 1386 (2°); Lega-Bartoccetti, *op. cit.*, *II*, n. 895, n. 5: "Si hic taceat antequam definiatur quaestio principalis, attentati revocationi censetur renunciasse. Id confirmatur expresse iure nostro quippe statuitur in p. 2ª h.c."

[21] Cf. Lega-Bartoccetti, as quoted in the previous note immediately *supra*.

[22] Cf. Roberti, *De Processibus*, I, n. 273; Coronata, *Institutiones*, III, n. 1211.

[23] Canon 1679 "... datur et, cuius interest, actio ad obtinendam

strained by the canons to petition for this remedy. It is declared that he possesses the right to do so. The decision whether such action is to be urged rests solely with the party as a rule. Though no express mention is made in canon 1855 of the possibility for the judge to act *ex officio*[24] in declaring the attempt null, nevertheless canon 1682 empowers him to do so in certain cases.[25] The cases which may require his intervention are: (1) the public good (e.g., nullity of a marriage, ordination; alienation of ecclesiastical property); (2) protection of the poor; (3) protection of minors.[26] Lega-Bartoccetti[27] state that in these cases the prejudicial attempts may be revoked not only by the judge *ex officio* but also at the request of the promoter of justice, or of the defender of the bond.

Ferreres[28] observed that the granted judicial action is an *actio rescissoria.*[29] This seems to be incorrect, since canon 1855, § 2, expressly states that the party is granted an "*actio ad obtinendam declarationem nullitatis.*" This same expression is found in canon 1679.[30] It is necessary only to declare (verify juridically) for the act the nullity which in virtue

declarationem nullitatis;" can. 1855, § 2 "... parti ex attentato laesae competit actio ad obtinendam declarationem nullitatis." Cf. can. 1682.

[24] Wernz-Vidal (*Ius Canonicum,* VI, n. 297) note here: "... per se in causis in quibus solius interest boni privati iudex non tenetur [relevare nullitatem ex officio], salva generali obligatione recte administrandi iustitiam ideoque procurandi observantiam legum processualium. . . ."

[25] Canon 1682.—Nullitas actus a iudice declarari non potest ex officio, nisi aut publice id intersit, aut agatur de pauperibus vel minoribus aliisve qui minorum iure censentur. Lega-Bartoccetti, *Commentarius,* II, n. 896, n. 5: " In aliis negotis *ex officio* a iudice vel ad instantiam promotoris iustitiae aut defensoris vinculi attentata revocantur."

[26] Cf. canons 88; 100, § 3.

[27] *Loc. cit.*

[28] *Institutiones Canonicae,* II, p. 337.

[29] Cf. canons 1684-1689. Roberti, *De Processibus,* I, n. 269 (IV, 1): "Rescindibilis dicitur actus qui valet, sed ob vitium quo laborat, auferri potest actione rescissori."

[30] Cf. note 23 of this article, *supra.*

of the law exists from the moment the attempt is committed. Noval[31] stated that the term *"attentatum"* is used in designation of an act which remains purely an attempt, since essentially (*per se*) it is juridically null and void. He then added that it is clear that the action is not an *actio rescissoria.*[32]

Article 3. The Competent Forum

The competent judge of the incidental cause for the declaration of the nullity of the prejudicial attempt is the judge who took cognizance of the principal cause.[33] Though the judge be the perpetrator of the attempt, he remains the competent judge. This fact is clear from the use of the words *"coram ipso iudice."*[34] If the party has reason to suspect the judge on account of the attempt, he may raise the exception of suspicion, which is to be decided according to canon 1615.[35] Accordingly the judge of the principal cause adjudicates the question of the attempt, even though he caused the prejudicial attempt, unless the exception of suspicion is lodged against him. Wernz-Vidal state that the

[31] *De Iudiciis*, nn. 602-603.

[32] *Op. cit.*, n. 603.

[33] Canon 1855, § 3.—"Actio haec instituenda est coram ipso iudice causae principalis"; Blat, *Commentarium*, Lib. IV, n. 380: "... *coram ipso iudice* primae vel secundae instantiae causam cognoscente ex propria competentia...." In the *Normae S. Romanae Rotae Tribunalis* (*AAS*, XXVI [1934] 449-492), art. 119, § 1, it is stated: "Actio ex attentato, ad obtinendam declarationem nullitatis, proponitur coram Turno." Bernardine (*Leges Processuales Vigentes*, Romae, 1947, p. 50) notes in regard to this article of the *Normae S.R.R.* that it is consonant with can. 1854 in that the question of a prejudicial attempt is an incidental question. The usage of the Rota, however, differs from the procedure in other incidental questions, since this question must be proposed directly before the *Turnus*. Cf. S.C. de Sacramentis, instr., *Provida Mater*, 15 aug. 1936, Art. 187-195—*AAS* XXVIII (1936), 349-350.

[34] Noval, *De Iudiciis*, n. 604: "... *coram ipso iudice etc.:* etiamsi attentatum commissum fuerit ab eodem."

[35] Canon 1855, § 3.—...quod si ob attentatum pars laesa iudicem suspectum habeat, exceptionem suspicionis potest opponere, in qua procedendum est ad normam can. 1615.

two incidental questions concerning the attempt and the suspicion of the judge are to be proposed jointly before the same tribunal.[36]

Coronata[37] and Goyeneche[38] discuss the variant opinions which hold that recourse is to be had to canon 1614, or to canon 1896, in regard to suspicion and the interpretation of canon 1855, § 3. Coronata bases his opinion upon that of Santamaria.[39] According to Coronata the Code does not refer to canon 1614, in which it is determined who shall decide the exception of suspicion against the judge. The reason for his silence is that, in order to regard the judge as suspect because of his attempt, it is sufficient that the injured party have lodged the exception of suspicion against him. The analogy that Coronata and Santamaria seem to draw between canon 1855, § 3, and canon 1896 is the following: in canon 1896 a party may request that another judge be substituted in his cause, if he fears that the judge's mind was prejudiced in pronouncing the sentence, which has been impugned with a plaint of nullity. For this reason the party would rightly hold the judge as suspect. *A fortiori,* the party injured by the attempt of the judge can thereby regard him as suspect.

Goyeneche, however, holds that canon 1855, § 3, seems rather to consider a common suspicion—not the special suspicion which a party may "rightly" hold, according to canon 1896, against the judge who pronounced the sentence.[40]

Canon 1855, § 3, states that the injured party can lodge

[36] *Ius Canonicum,* VI, n. 574: "Facile tamen fieri poterit, ubi attentatum ab ipso iudice procedat, ut hic parti fiat rationabiliter suspectus: in tali casu simul cum incidenti causa attentati proponitur incidens causa recusationis iudicis."

[37] *Institutiones,* III, n. 1386 (2° at note 7).

[38] *De Processibus,* I, pt. 2, p. 132.

[39] Cf. *Comentarios ad Código Canónico* (6 vols., Madrid, 1919-1922), V, n. 222.

[40] *Loc. cit.:* "Alii putant, in casu non esse recurrendum ad can. 1614, sed potius ad c. 1896, vi cuius possit pars exigere absque alio, si suspectum habeat iudicem ob attentatum, ut alius iudex in eodem tamen sede subrogetur ad normam c. 1615. E contra videtur hic agi

an exception of suspicion, if he should suspect the judge by reason of the attempt. It seems, therefore, that the Code does not absolutely identify the judge's prejudicial attempt with his being simultaneously suspect. A judge may be suspect for many reasons other than the fact that he committed the attempt.[41] It is to be concluded, then, that the judge does not become suspect simply for the reason that he has committed a prejudicial attempt. It follows, therefore, that the question of suspicion is to be decided according to canon 1614.

Once the accusation has been formally lodged, the trial regarding the alleged suspicion must be prosecuted with the utmost dispatch (*expeditissime*).[42] Moreover, the parties and also the promoter of justice and the defender of the bond must be heard, if these officials have an interest in the cause and are not themselves suspect.[43] The party may join the exception of suspicion with the judicial action to obtain a declaration of nullity of the attempt. The petition is proposed orally or in writing.[44] In the petition the following facts must receive mention: (1) the act to which the accusation refers; (2) the person accused, and (3) the reason for the accusation.

The judge assigns the shortest terms[45] possible for the presentation of the proof.[46] After a short defence has been presented, the incidental question of suspicion is defined

de suspicione communi, non de illa speciali quam potest 'merito' habere iuxta c. 1896 contra iudicem qui sententiam tulit."

[41] Cf. canon 1613, § 1; Roberti, *De Processibus*, I, n. 172 (II, 1). Wernz-Vidal (*Ius Canonicum*, VI, n. 147) reduce the reasons for a just suspicion to four: "I. Directum vel indirectum interesse iudicis in causa. II. Praesumptus specialis affectus iudicis erga unam partem. III. Praesumptum odium seu inimicitia iudicis erga unam partem. IV. Praeiudicium a iudice conceptum propter ipsius praecedentem interventum in eadem causa."

[42] Canon 1616; cf. can. 1880, 7°.

[43] Canon 1616.

[44] Canon 1838.

[45] Cf. canons 1616 and 1634-1635.

[46] Canon 1840, § 2.

by means of a decree in which the reasons *in facto* and *in iure* are set down briefly.[47] The decision of the judge is then communicated to the parties and to the promoter of justice and the defender of the bond, if they participated in the cause. There is no appeal from the decision rendered on the question of suspicion.[48]

The effects of the judicially proposed incidental question of suspicion are these:[49] (1) the principal cause is suspended and the judge must refrain from further action in the cause, until the question of suspicion has been decided; (2) once the question is settled, two possibilities arise: a) if the decision favored the judge, he continues with the principal cause; b) if the decision went against him, he must be replaced with a judge who remains above suspicion.[50] Though a substitution of judges is to be made, no change results for the hearing of the cause in its original instance.[51]

In his discussion of the question of suspicion, Roberti[52] proposes the problem whether acts placed by a suspect judge are valid. He notes that some authors hold that such are null *ipso iure* by reason of the nature of the prejudicial question.[53] Others are of the opinion that the validity of these acts depends on the outcome of the incidental question.[54] Roberti concludes that the first opinion seems to be more reasonable. He bases his conclusion on two arguments: (1) if there is no judge, then a condition essential for the further prosecution of the process seems lacking; (2) an act placed by a judge so charged very often constitutes a prejudicial attempt.[55]

[47] Canon 1840, §§ 2, 3. [48] Cf. canons 1880, 7°; 1616.

[49] Cf. Roberti, *De Processibus*, I, n. 173 (V).

[50] Cf. canon 1615, §§ 2, 3. [51] Canon 1615, § 1.

[52] *De Processibus*, I, n. 173 (V).

[53] Cf. Lega-Bartoccetti, *Commentarius*, I, p. 229, nn. 2-3.

[54] Cf. Reiffenstuel, *Ius Canonicum*, Lib. II, tit. 28, n. 326; Pirhing, *Ius Canonicum*, Lib. II, tit. 28, n. 277; Santi, *Praelectiones*, Lib. II, tit. 28, n. 52; Coronata, *Institutiones*, III, n. 1146 (6°, note 7).

[55] Cf. canons 1854 and 1855.

CHAPTER VI

PROCEDURE IN DECLARING THE NULLITY OF A PREJUDICIAL ATTEMPT[1]

ARTICLE 1. SOLUTION OF THE INCIDENTAL QUESTION OF AN *Attentatum*[2]

A prejudicial attempt reflects one of the three categories which under the heading of incidental questions are given detailed consideration in Book IV, Title XI of the Code.[3] For a determination of the proper mode of procedure to be employed in the matter of declaring the nullity of an attempt, canons 1837-1841 must be joined with canon 1856.[4] An incidental cause is a question which is proposed by one of the parties (or perhaps by the promoter of justice or the defender of the bond, if they are participating in the trial),[5] after the trial has opened in view of the previously effected citation.[6] This question, though not mentioned expressly in the bill of complaint (*libellus*), must be so connected with the principal cause that as a rule it must be resolved before the principal question itself can yield to

[1] Canon 1856.—§ 1. Pendente quaestione de attentato, cursus causae principalis regulariter suspenditur, sed si iudici opportunius videatur, questio de attentato potest una cum causa principali pertractari et resolvi.

§ 2. Quaestiones de attentatis expeditissime sunt pertractandae et decreto iudicis definiendae, auditis partibus et promotore iustitiae vel defensore vinculi, si hi iudicio intersint.

[2] Cf. Wernz-Vidal, *Ius Canonicum,* VI, n. 575; Lega-Bartoccetti, *Commentarius,* II, 896 f.; Noval, *De Iudiciis,* n. 604; Roberti, *De Processibus,* II, n. 433; Coronata, *Institutiones,* III, n. 1386 (3°); Cappello, *Summa Iuris Canonici,* III, n. 299.

[3] Cf. canons 1837-1857. S.C. de Sacramentis, instr., *Provida Mater,* 15 aug. 1936, Art. 187-195—*AAS,* XXVIII (1936), 349-350.

[4] Cf. Lega-Bartoccetti, *op. cit.,* II, 896, n. 8; canons 1627-1633.

[5] Cf. canon 1837.

[6] Cf. canon 1725, 5°.

a solution.[7] It is readily seen, therefore, that the general rules pertaining to incidental questions are to be applied in the process of declaring an attempt null. If the canons on prejudicial attempts determine a particular mode of procedure, then it will take precedence. Coronata notes that, though it is generally left to the judge to determine whether an incidental cause is to be treated in the more formal judicial manner or administratively, causes involving prejudicial attempts are to be adjudicated adminstratively.[8]

The judicial action for the declaration of the nullity of the attempt is introduced by way of a written bill of complaint or by means of an oral petition.[9] If the petition is made orally, it should immediately be put into writing by the notary.[10] The connection which the incidental question has with the principal cause must be indicated in the bill of complaint. In so far as it is possible, the prescriptions of canons 1706-1725 on the introduction of a cause are to be observed. After the judge has received the written or oral petition, he hears the parties as well as the promoter of justice or the defender of the bond, if they are participating in the trial. He then decides whether the incidental question is futile and raised merely to delay the prosecution of the principal cause.[11] Such futility and dilatoriness is the danger presented by incidental questions, especially if it reflects a party's incrimination with a prejudicial attempt.

If the incidental question is found to be connected with the principal cause and has a probable basis, the judge or the tribunal shall then admit the question by a special de-

[7] Cf. canons 1837, 1856.

[8] *Institutiones*, III, n. 1386 (3°). Cf. Goyeneche, *De Processibus*, I, pt. 2, p. 133.

[9] Canon 1838. This petition may also be made by the promoter of justice or by the defender of the bond according to canon 1682.

[10] Cf. canon 1707, § 3.

[11] Canon 1839. Cf. S.C. de Sacramentis, instr., *Provida Mater*, 15 aug. 1936, Art. 189, § 1—*AAS*, XXVIII (1936), 349.

cree; otherwise, if these two requisites[12] do not coexist, the judge should reject the petition by his decree. Upon the acceptance of the incidental question, the judge shall determine the time when it shall be adjudicated.[13]

Canons 1837 and 1839 give the judge complete discretion in determining whether an incidental question is so related to the principal cause that it must be resolved before the principal cause itself. However, canon 1856, § 1,[14] gives preference to an immediate decision, prior to the solution of the principal cause, by stating that the question of a prejudicial attempt regularly suspends the course of the principal cause. Among the reasons which one could advance for this procedure, one could mention the following: the urgency to repair (1) the damage caused by a prejudicial attempt, and (2) the *ipso iure* effected nullity of the attempt, which, if it were not removed, would affect the remainder of the procedure of the principal cause.[15] The judge, if he deems it more opportune, may decide to resolve the incidental question along with the principal cause.[16] As an example, the reason for postponing the solution of the incidental question could well be the fact that only thus

[12] Cf. S.C. de Sacramentis, instr., *Provida Mater*, 15 aug. 1936, Art. 189, § 2—*AAS*, XXVIII (1936), 349. Canon 1839.

[13] Cf. canon 1839 and 1840, § 2. S.C. de Sacramentis, instr., *Provida Mater*, 15 aug. 1936, Art. 189, § 2, and 191—*AAS*, XXVIII (1936), 349-350.

[14] "Pendente quaestione de attentato, cursus causae principalis regulariter suspenditur, sed si iudici opportunius videatur, quaestio de attentato potest una cum causa principali pertractari et resolvi."

[15] Cf. *supra*, page 122. Noval, *De Iudiciis*, n. 604: "... *regulariter:* quia si revera actus fuit attentatorium, et proinde nullus, frustra continuatur processus in causa principalis qui devenit invalidus." Jone, *Commentarium in Codicem Iuris Canonici* (3 vols., Paderborn: Officia Libraria F. Schnoeningh, 1950-1955), III, 204: "Si haec attentata postea non fuerunt sanata, *sententia,* quae nititur his attentatis, est nulla ad normam can. 1680, § 2." Hanssen, "De sanctione nullitatis in processu canonico," *Apollinaris,* XI (1938), 402 f.; Ciprotti, "De novis probationibus post conclusionem in causa," *Apollinaris,* XII (1939), 111.

[16] Canon 1856, § 1.

does it become possible to collect more information on the attempt without interrupting the course of the principal cause.[17]

If incidental causes are generally considered, canon 1840, § 1, states that it is left to the judge's discretion whether, in view of the nature and the gravity of the matter, the question shall be decided in a formal trial by interlocutory sentence or by a decree of the judge.[18] Canon 1856, however, imposes the administrative process, which is to be concluded with the decree of the judge.[19] Among the possible reasons which might be adduced for this mode of procedure is the necessity—even an extreme urgency—of repairing the injury of the prejudicial attempt. There is also the expediency of avoiding delaying maneuvers. All dispatch, therefore, is to be used in processing the incidental question.[20] Nevertheless, all the essential forms of justice must be preserved: the hearing of the parties, of the promoter of justice, and of the defender of the bond (can. 1856, § 2).

The burden of proof of the invalidity of the attempt rests with the plaintiff in the incidental question. He must prove the fact which constitutes the innovation and the damage

[17] Lega-Bartoccetti, *Commentarius*, II, 897, n. 8: "Ast cavet ipse textus legis, id contingere '*regulariter*'; quia sunt casus exceptionis, veluti, quoties ipsius spoliati interest, ob naturam attentati, expetere a iudice ne tractationem suspendat causae principalis, ut puta, si agatur de proprietate fundi et reus conventus partem alienat fundi in quam ipse contendit, nullimode cadere proprietatis quaestionem. Expedit hoc in casu principalem quaestionem non suppendere sed hanc definire et una simul in sententia definitiva edicere an attentatum patratum fuerit et quomodo sit revocandum." Cf. Noval, *De Iudiciis*, n. 604; S.C. de Sacramentis, instr., 15 aug. 1936, Art. 194—*AAS*, XXVIII (1936), 350; Doheny, *Canonical Procedure*, I, 154.

[18] Cf. S.C. de Sacramentis, instr., *Provida Mater*, 15 aug. 1936, Art. 190, § 1—*AAS*, XXVIII (1936), 349.

[19] Canon 1856, § 2.—Quaestiones de attentatis expeditissime sunt pertractandae et decreto iudicis definiendae, auditis partibus et promotore iustitiae vel defensore vinculi, si hi iudicio intersint.

[20] Canon 1856, § 2: "expeditissime." Cf. also canons 1616; 1709, § 3; 1852, § 3; Noval, *De Iudiciis*, n. 604.

which ensued.[21] The clause "*demonstrato attentato*" of canon 1857 recalls that there is question of a purely declaratory decision, proclaiming the nullity *ipso iure* of the act recognized as a prejudicial attempt. If the attempt is not proved, the questioned act remains valid.[22]

No appeal is granted from the judge's decree which decides the question of the attempt.[23] Lega-Bartoccetti[24] state that the requirement of defining the question of the attempt by a decree does not imply that it is not a judicial definition. It signifies, rather, that there is no place for an appeal, and the process must be expedited by the use of short delays (terms).[25]

Indeed, everyone realizes what serious detriment (*praeiudicium*) would be inflicted upon an injured party and upon the due cognizance of trials, if a cause involving an attempt, though suspending the principal cause, would not be treated with the necessary dispatch. If the prinicpal

[21] Roberti, *De Processibus*, II, n. 433. Wernz-Vidal, *Ius Canonicum*, VI, n. 575 (3°): "... incidentem causam movens nihil aliud tenetur probare nisi factum attentati, nam dissensus supponitur ubi agitur de facto nocivo, ac proinde pars quae incusatur de attentato debet probare alterius partis consensum. Quodsi attentatum fuit cognitum parti cui nocebat, et haec tacuit, praesumptione, quae tamen admittat contrariam probationem, censebitur sui iuri renuntiasse et consensisse, nisi contra dissemulationem attentati obstet ratio boni publici." Lega-Bartoccetti, *Commentarius*, II, 866, n. 6: "Instantia qua vero petitur declaratio, continere debet probationem: 1) de *inhibitione* legitime cognita seu denunciata alteri parti, atque 2) de *laesione* inde secuta eiusdem inhibitionis.—Quare si probatio neque *unum* neque *alterum* evincat, iudex respuit instantiam incidentalem."

[22] Wernz-Vidal, *loc. cit.;* Cocchi, *Commentarium*, VII, 334: "Si attentatum plene non probetur, standum est pro valore actus."

[23] Canon 1856, § 2: "expeditissime"; canon 1880: "Non est locus appellationi: ... 7° A sententia in causa pro qua ius cavet expeditissime rem esse definiedam." Cf. Roberti, *De Processibus*, II, n. 433; Coronata, *Institutiones*, III, n. 1386 (3°); Goyeneche, *De Processibus*, I, pt. 2, p. 133.

[24] *Commentarius*, II, 897, n. 9: "Definiri quaestionem decreto, non secumfert definitionem non esse iudicialem; sed significat non esse locum appelationi et processum debere brevibus dilationibus expediri."

[25] Cf. canons 1634-1635.

cause is appealed, the question of the prejudicial attempt may again be proposed, so that there can be removed whatever injurious burden it may have imposed. This renewed proposal of the incidental question of the attempt can be made in the appeal, although a decree has defined the matter of an attempt in the first instance. There arises simply a new complaint—not the revision of the decree in an appeal—or a new redress.[26]

The decree that is to be issued by the judge[27] is not an interlocutory sentence, and, therefore, in form it is not strictly judicial.[28] Here it is evident that the decree is to be employed when the hearing of the principal cause is suspended for the settling of the incidental question. There is a doubt, however, whether this same decree is to be used if the incidental question is decided along with the principal cause itself.[29] A solution to this problem is presented by Article 194 of the Instruction, *Provida Mater.*[30] This Article of the *Instructio* states that the incidental question and the principal cause may well be decided in one and the same sentence, if the cause so suggests. The question of an attempt has by its very definition[31] a close relationship with the principal cause. Consequently, it will not be necessary to issue both a decree and a sentence at the end of the trial, if the incidental question is then resolved, since the decision on the attempt can easily be incorporated into the definitive

[26] Lega-Bartoccetti, *loc. cit.:* "Hac de causa non admittitur appellatio, ex can. 1880, 7°. In gradu autem appellationis cum agitur de principali quaestione, iterum moveri potest quaestio de attentato ut eius gravamen removeatur etsi per *decretum* causa de attentato in prima instantia, definita sit. Est nova querela, non revisio decreti in gradu appellationis, aut recursus." Cf. canon 1841; 1880, 6°.

[27] Cf. canon 1856, § 2.

[28] Noval, *De Iudiciis*, n. 604: "*...et decreto:* non sententia interlocutoria, et proinde non in forma stricte iudiciali."

[29] Canon 1856, § 1. "...si iudici opportunius videatur, quaestio de attentato potest una cum causa principali pertractari et resolvi."

[30] S.C. de Sacramentis, instr., *Provida Mater*, 15 aug. 1936—*AAS*, XXVIII (1936), 350.

[31] Cf. canon 1854.

sentence itself. Such a procedure is implied in canons 1839 and 1856, § 1.[32] Lega-Bartoccetti[33] are also of the opinion that the incidental question, if the principal cause is not suspended, should be defined along with the definitive sentence of the principal cause according to canon 1856, § 1.

The decree which defines the incidental question, when the principal cause has been suspended for its adjudication, is one that abstracts from the formalities of a sentence properly so-called.[34]

According to canon 1840, § 3,[35] the decree shall contain the reasons *in facto* and *in iure* briefly set down. The decree is to contain these reasons whether the incidental question is rejected or defined. Coronata[36] sagely remarks that the requirement for a brief exposition of the reasons, as based on fact and on law, is well put, so that the judge will not suppose that he can settle the matter with a purely arbitrary act of his own.

Since the law is insistent that the factual and legal reasons for the judge's decision are to be expressed in the decree,[37] and that the incidental question is to be settled with the utmost dispatch (*expeditissime*), it can be concluded that moral certitude[38] is necessary for the decree as well as the sentence.[39] The reason for this is that a decree which

[32] Cf. S.C. de Sacramentis, instr., *Provida Mater*, 15 aug. 1936, Art. 189, § 2—*AAS*, XXVIII (1936), 349. Torre, *Processus Matrimonialis*, p. 323; Doheny, *Canonical Procedure*, I, 462.

[33] *Commentarius*, II, 897, n. 9: "At sententia definiretur nempe per sententiam principalis causae definitivam ad mentem P. 1ae, *quoties causa ... potest una cum principali pertractari et resolvi.*"

[34] Canon 1840, § 3. "... non servata iudicii forma."

[35] Cf. S.C. de Sacramentis, instr., *Provida Mater*, 15 aug. 1936, Art. 193—*AAS*, XXVIII (1936), 350.

[36] *Institutiones*, III, n. 1372 (a): "... rectissime factum est ne iudex putet suo mero arbitrio se rem dirimere posse."

[37] Cf. canons 1840, § 3; 1873, § 1, 3°.

[38] Cf. canons 1869; 1873, § 1, 3°.

[39] In regard to the moral certitude required for a sentence, the following may be consulted: *Allocutio* of Pope Pius XII, *AAS*, XXXIV (1942), 338-343. Torre, *Processus Matrimonialis*, p. 529; McCarthy,

defines an incidental question[40] is not substantially different from an interlocutory sentence. Thus, since moral certitude is required for an interlocutory sentence,[41] it is also necessary for a decree which is pronounced upon a incidental question.

If the incidental question is decided together with the definitive sentence pronounced upon the principal cause, there can be no doubt that the law requires moral certitude for the matter that is to be defined by the sentence. Since canon 1856, § 2, prescribes that the judge is to define the incidental question of an attempt by means of a decree, then a sentence which defines both the principal cause and the incidental cause must have moral certitude as its basis for the definition of both causes. The purpose of the law is to protect the rights of the parties in all eventualities. The judge, therefore, in pronouncing the decree upon the incidental question, when the principal cause has been suspended, must be motivated not by arbitrariness, but by moral certitude derived from reasons deduced from the facts and the law.

The form of the decree will follow this general outline: (1) the word "decree" is employed; (2) the name of the judge (or judges) and his qualifications are related; (3) the cause which occasions the decree is set down; (4) some indication shows whether the judicial action was begun *ex officio* or at the request of the party; (5) the dispositive part

De Certitudine Morali Quae in Iudicis Animo ad Sententiae Pronuntiationem Requiritur (Rome: Catholic Book Agency, 1948).

[40] Roberti, *De Processibus*, I (4. ed.), n. 205 (II, 1): "Possumus distinguere decreta *decisoria* et *ordinatoria*, prout diriguntur ad definiendam quaestionem incidentem, vel ad moderandum processus. 2. Decreta decisoria dantur, loco sententiae, pro iudicis arbitrio, ad solvendas quaestiones incidentes minus graves . . . , nisi appareant futiles et ad retardandum processum unice excitatae, quo in casu iudex potest quoque simplici decreto ordinatorio reiicere. . . ."

[41] Canon 1869, § 1.—Ad pronuntiationem cuiuslibet sententiae requiritur in iudicis animo moralis certitudo circa rem sententia definiendam.

as the conclusion from reasons in fact and in law is briefly set out; (6) the place, day, month and year are indicated (they can be put at the beginning or at the end of the decree); (7) the judge and the notary sign the decree, and (8), if damages are to be paid, the amount is determined in the decree also.[42]

If the decree was issued prior to the sentence which defines the principal cause, the judge may reverse his decision before this sentence, in order to correct it or revoke it: (1) on his own accord, after hearing the parties, or (2) at the request of a party, after hearing the other party, with the advice of the promoter of justice or defender of the bond.[43] Lega-Bartoccetti note the fact that canon 1841 makes no express mention of the correction or revocation of the decree. Though this be so, they concluded that *a fortiori* it must be admitted that the judge can revoke or correct his decree. They base their conclusion upon a rule of law, namely, "if what is greater is lawful for a person, then, indeed, he is permitted the lesser."[44]

The correction may be done at the request of the promoter of justice or of the defnder of the bond. Even though the promoter of justice (defender of the bond) does not request the judge to act, nevertheless the canon[45] demands that their advice should be obtained, if they are present at the proceedings. Lega-Bartoccetti note that, if they are not consulted, the decree is nonetheless valid.[46]

[42] Cf. canons 1856; 1857; 1874; 1840, § 3. Roberti, *De Processibus*, I, n. 205 (II, 2).

[43] Canon 1841.

[44] *Commentarius*, II, 860, n. 12. In the 1950 printing of the *Commentarius* of Lega-Bartoccetti (*ibid.*, note 2) the number of this rule is incorrect. The rule referred to is n. 53 instead of n. 21. Reg. 53, R.J., in VI°: "Cui licet quod est plus licet quod est minus." Reg. 35, R.J., in VI° is also applicable here: "Plus semper in se continet quod est minus." Cf. Bartoccetti, *De Regulis Iuris Canonici*, pages 193 f, 145 f respectively, for a detailed consideration of these rules of law.

[45] Canon 1841.

Article 2. Juridic Effects of a Demonstrated *Attentatum*[47]

Section A. Revocation of the *Attentatum*

Once the prejudicial attempt is demonstrated, its revocation is to be decreed in all cases, since there is question of an act null *ipso iure,* and not of one annulled by the decree of the judge.[48] Thus, by the decree of the judge, what never effectually existed in law will no longer exist in fact. The revocation or purgation of an attempt consists in the restoration of the object or the matter to the status it had prior to the occurrence of the attempt during the pending litigation.[49] The revocation of the attempt is enjoined in the same decree which declared the nullity of the attempt. There is no need for two separate decrees. This fact is evident from a comparison of canon 1856, § 2, with canon 1857. Therefore, if the litigious matter was alienated through the prejudicial aattempt, it must be restored to the plaintiff of the incidental question; if it cannot be restored, its equivalent must be substituted.[50]

Lega-Bartoccetti state that a prejudicial attempt is a species of spoliation (*spolium*).[51] The rule of the *exceptio*

[46] *Commentarius,* III, 860, n. 12, note 3: "Si non audiantur nihilominus tenet decretum." In regard to this matter, the opposite opinion, namely, that the decree would not be valid, is tenable. Cf. canons 105 and 1587, § 1.

[47] Canon 1857.—§ 1. Demonstrato attentato, iudex decernere debet eius revocationem seu purgationem.

§ 2. Quod si attentatum vi vel dolo patratum sit, qui illud commisit, tenetur etiam de damnis erga partem laesam.

[48] Canon 1857, § 1. "... decernere debet...."

[49] Noval, *De Iudiciis,* n. 605: "... *revocationem:* id est, omnium rerum restitutionem in eum statum quo erant ante attentatum." Lega-Bartoccetti, *Commentarius,* II, 898, n. 10: "... revocari ... attentatum significat rem in pristinum statum restitui...." Coronata, *Institutiones,* III, n. 1386 (4°): "... in pristinum statum, ad statum nempe in quo res ante innovationem factam lite pendente inveniebatur." Cf. *supra,* page 37 ff.

[50] Reiffenstuel, *Ius Canonicum,* Lib. II, tit. 16, nn. 34 ff.

[51] *Commentarius,* II, 894, n. 2: "... patet attentatum esse speciem

spolii then applies:[52] the one spoliated (despoiled) need only prove the fact of spoliation to recover the possession.[53] While waiting for the restitution of the litigious object, at least by sequestration, the one spoliated in consequence of the prejudicial attempt is not required to appear in court or to place any judicial act, in order that the trial may otherwise proceed, unless the restoration is suspended judicially for some cause. Though the person deprived of possession or quasi-possession when brought into court has the right to be reinstated in possession before the hearing of the cause proceeds, still the judge may at the request of the other party or of the promoter of justice decree that the reinstatement be suspended, or that the object or person be put into the custody of a sequester until the end of the trial, if there is danger in the restitution of this object or right.[54] An example of such danger would be the cruel treatment of a wife by the husband, if he demanded the resumption of conjugal consortium.[55]

As to the relationship between a cause involving a prejudicial attempt and a cause of spoliation, Cardinal Tuschus (d. 1620) regarded the cause of prejudicial attempts more privileged and having more favor before the law. He reasoned that in a cause of spoliation the injured party received back only the object which had been taken after the trial was over; in a cause of a prejudicial attempt, the injured party recovered the object of the controversy for the remainder of the trial. This party was also to retain the liti-

spolii, quia alium deturbat a pacifica quasi-possessione sui iuris, ad normam can. 1689, p. 1." Noval, *De Iudiciis,* n. 605: "In hac parte attentatum est species spolii: et hoc adeo verum est 'ut antequam innovata revocentur, parte opponente impediatur processus ad ulteriora.'" Cf. Reiffenstuel, *op. cit.,* Lib. II, tit. 16, n. 36; Roberti, *De Processibus,* I, nn. 292 ff.; Coronata, *Institutiones,* III, nn. 1228 ff.

[52] Canon 1699, § 1.

[53] Canon 1699, § 2.

[54] Cf. canons 1699, § 3; 1854; 1672; 1673.

[55] Cf. canon 1699, § 3.

gious object in his possession, provided that the sentence was pronounced in his behalf.[56]

SECTION B. COMPENSATION FOR LOSS OR INJURY SUSTAINED[57]

In certain cases the party injured by the prejudicial attempt is granted compensation by the law. Thus, canon 1857, § 2, prescribes that, if the attempt was made through violence or fraud, the person guilty of the attempt is constrained to indemnify the injured party. No provision is otherwise made for compensation, namely, if the attempt was committed without violence or fraud. Nor is there any indication as to how the amount of the compensation is to be determined.[58]

Though an attempt is always null *ipso iure,*[59] it is not always culpable,[60] that is, stained with violence or fraud. Only when force (*vis*)[61] has been used or an injurious maneuver (*dolus*)[62] has been perpetrated, is there any

[56] *Practicae Conclusiones Iuris,* I, concl. 548, p. 273. Cf. *supra,* page 19.

[57] Canon 1857, § 2.

[58] The Oriental Code (Pius XII, Motu Proprio, *Sollicitudinem Nostram,* 6 ian. 1950—*AAS,* XLII [1950], 5-120) has excluded any reference in canon 381 to compensation for an attempt committed through violence or fraud. The other canons of the Oriental Code on prejudicial attempts (can. 378-380) are worded the same as those in the Latin Code (can. 1854-1857).

[59] Canon 1855, § 1.

[60] Roberti, *De Processibus,* II, n. 432 (b): "Damna quoque parti laesae sunt sarcienda si attentatum vi aut dolo patratum sit. . . . Ex hoc confirmatur haberi posse attentatum etiam ex actu bona fide posito, dummodo praeiudicium attulerit." Torquebiau-Noz-De Clercq-Jombart, *Traité de Droit Canonique* (4 vols., Vol. IV, Letouzey et Ané, Paris, 1949), IV, 324: "L'innovation doit avoir pour résultat un prejudice (ce qui n'implique pas nécessairement la mauvaise foi de son auteur) . . ."

[61] Noval, *De Iudiciis,* n. 605: ". . . *vi:* veluti si pars, contra voluntatem alterius, colligeret fructus fundi ab ista possessi." Lega-Bartoccetti, *Commentarius,* II, 898, n. 10: "Praeterae si in attentato adhibita fuerit violentia . . . , damnatur pars attentans . . . damnum emergens ex ipsa causa violenti."

[62] Coronata, *Institutiones,* III, n. 1386 (4°): "Dolus autem hic accipitur pro male fide quae intervenis in attentatis ponendis." Noval,

necessity for exacting compensation (damages)[63] from the culprit in favor of the injured party.[64] An example of force is the rapine of the thing contested or its fruits; of fraud, (a) the sale of the litigious object to a person more powerful than the first possessor, or (b) the alienation of a controverted right to one who then takes the matter to another jurisdiction (such as the civil jurisdiction), so that the trial becomes more difficult for the other party.

When damages are to be paid, the judge determines the amount.[65] Augustine[66] makes this observation on the amount of damages to be paid: "The perpetrators are bound to indemnify the injured party to an amount corresponding to the period beginning at the time when the action was brought up to the moment of its settlement. This indemnification includes expenses as well as the revenues received or gain made during this time."[67] Therefore, if compensa-

De Iudiciis, n. 605: "...*dolo:* ut si litigans alienasset rem, nulla conservationis eiusdem cogente necessitate aut suadente utilitate, sed eo consilio ut deveniret in manus potentioris personae, utputa advocato; aut vendidisset vel donasset actionem personae, quae eam pertractatura est coram alio tribunali, v.g., tribunali laico, unde lis alteri parti durior aut difficilior fiat." Cf. S.R.R., *Decisiones*, XXIX (1937), Dec. LX, p. 597, n. 5.

[63] Lega-Bartoccetti, *Commentarius*, II, 898: "Nomine *damni* venit lucrum cessans aut damnum emergens ex ipsa causa violenti aut dolosi attentati: et hoc nomine venire etiam *fructus* non est ambigendum."

[64] C. 2, X, *de dolo et contumacia*, II, 14: "... nos attendentes malitiam et dolum nulli patrocinari debere ... mandamus. ..."

[65] Canon 1873, § 1. Cappello, *Summa Iuris Canonici*, III, 249, n. 4: "Quantitas reparationis damnorum a iudice est aestimanda. Si iudex ipse attentatum commiserit, recurrendum est ad iudicem appllationis." Cf. Noval, *De Iudiciis*, n. 605.

[66] *A Commentary*, VII, 300.

[67] This statement of Augustine *(loc. cit.)* seems to be based on can. 1731, 3°. The canon cited, however, does not appear to be applicable here, since indemnification is to be made from the moment the prejudicial attempt took place. The prejudicial atempt may well have been committed prior to the joinder of issue, which is the *terminus a quo* of computation in can. 1731, 3°. Just as restoration of the litigious matter must be made *ad statum quo ante*, so also must any determination of the amount of indemnification be reckoned accordingly.

tion is to be given to the injured party by reason of the extant fraud or violence, the judge will make provision to this effect in his decree: he will pronounce that a certain amount of damages is to be paid to the injured party.

No further mention is made in canon 1857 of the expenses which are ordinarily incurred in the adjudication of the incidental question itself. This consideration enters regardless of whether the attempt has been committed through violence or fraud. This does not imply that the usual expenses incurred in the trial are not to be provided for according to the general prescriptions of the canons in regard to judicial expenses.[68] Canon 1681 states that the person placing an act vitiated with nullity is bound to pay damages and expenses to the injured party. Along with this canon, canon 1910, § 1, is to be read: the party who loses the incidental cause must as a rule repay the judicial expenses to the winner.[69]

Lega-Bartoccetti note that, if the perpetrator of the prejudicial attempt acted in good faith, he will be bound only to the expenses which it would be unjust for the injured party to bear, even though fraud was lacking in the attempt. If the injured party suffered damages from the attempt (provided they were not the result of a mere misfortune), it is also unjust that he be made to bear them, even though the perpetrator did not act through fraud or violence.[70]

In virtue of canon 1681, the decree of the judge will, therefore, require the defendant to pay the expenses that were incurred by reason of the prejudicial attempt, regardless of whether an additional amount is exacted in damages for violence or fraud itself in this matter.

[68] Cf. canons 1908-1916, 1681.

[69] "Victus victori iudiciales expensas regulariter reficere tenetur . . . in causa . . . incidenti." Roberti, *De Processibus,* II, n. 432 (a): "Pars quae attentatum commisit tenetur expensas huius phasis processualis solvere." Cf. Goyeneche, *De Processibus,* I, pt. 2, p. 133.

[70] *Commentarius,* II, 898: "Hoc sensu semper pro parte laesa locus est refectioni *expensarum* etiam non iudicialium."

There is one final sanction to be noted in the discussion of prejudicial attempts. If the attempt itself constitutes a crime, the judge and the ministers of the tribunal[71] as well as the parties[72] can be punished.[73]

[71] Cf. canon 1625, §§ 1, 3.

[72] Cf. canons 1640, § 2; 1743, § 3.

[73] Cf. Roberti, *De Processibus*, II, n. 432 (c); Marchesi, *Summula Iuris Canonici*, IV, 179; Giménez Fernandez, *Instituciones Juridicas*, II, 263.

CONCLUSIONS

1. The edictal citation is to be understood as having been legitimately intimated to the defendant according to canon 1725 after there has elapsed the predetermined time during which the judge has arranged for it to be affixed to the chancery doors and to be published in a newspaper (diocesan or secular). (p. 64)

2. If the joinder of issue (*litis contestatio*) is omitted, the termination of the pending of the litigation will be governed by the canons regulating the abatement of a lawsiut. (p. 74)

3. If the instance is interrupted according to canon 1733, 1°, the pending of the litigation continues and will not be affected by any abatement. The period of abatement will begin to run only after it is ascertained that the heir or successor spoken of in this canon has become able to proceed with the trial according to canon 1736. (pp. 77 f.)

4. A decree or a simple interlocutory sentence has no effect upon the pending of the litigation, even though an appeal is denied according to canon 1880, 6°. An interlocutory sentence with definitive force prolongs the pending of the litigation, if an appeal can be expected according to canons 1881, 1883, 1886, 1889, 1902, 2°. (pp. 83 f.)

5. The pending of the litigation is terminated in the following ways: (1) by the controverted object's becoming an adjudged issue (*res iudicata*); (2) by a settlement (*transactio*); (3) by a deputized arbitration; (4) by a decision-entailing oath; (5) by the application of canon 1850, § 3, against a plaintiff guilty of contempt of court; (6) by the abatement of the lawsuit; (7) by a renunciation of the lawsuit, and (8) by an extinction or quashing of the lawsuit. (pp. 79 ff.)

6. In matrimonial causes, canon 1987 (cf. also can. 1996) supposes that the defender of the bond may always appeal

within ten days, after two concordant sentences, and leaves the decision to appeal solely to his conscience. It is necessary to wait these ten days to allow the defender to deliberate and thereupon to declare that he will not appeal, in order that after this time-limit (*terminus*) one can consider the pending of the litigation as having ceased. If the defender permits the ten days to expire without interposing an appeal, or if he declares that he will not interpose it, the pending of the litigation ceases through the renunciation of the appeal. (p. 93)

7. A judge who commits a prejudicial attempt does not by that fact alone become suspect. (p. 136)

8. The decree by means of which the judge defines the incidental question of a prejudicial attempt must be based on moral certitude. (pp. 144 f.)

BIBLIOGRAPHY

SOURCES

Acta Apostolica Sedis, Commentarium Officiale, Romae, 1909—.

Codex Iuris Canonici, Pii X Pontificis Maximi iussu digestus, Benedicti Papae XV auctoritate promulgatus, Praefatione, Fontium Annotatione et Indice Analytico-Alphabetico, ab Emo Petri Card. Gasparri Auctus, Romae: Typis Polyglottis Vaticanis, 1917; Reimpressio, 1949.

Codicis Iuris Canonici Fontes, cura Emi Petri Card. Gasparri editi, 9 vols., Romae (postea Civitate Vaticana): Typis Polyglottis Vaticanis, 1923-1939 (Vols. VII-IX, ed. cura et studio Emi Iustiniani Card. Serédi).

Corpus Iuris Canonici, 2 ed., Lipsiensis, post Aemilii Ludovici Richteri curas instruxit Aemilius Friedberg, 2 vols., Lipsiae, 1879-1881.

Corpus Iuris Civilis, Vol. I, *Institutiones*—recognovit P. Krueger; *Digesta*—recognovit Theodorus Mommsen, retractavit P. Krueger; Vol. II, *Codex Iustinianus*—recognovit et retractavit P. Krueger; Vol. III, *Novellae Constitutiones*—recognovit R. Schoell, opus Schoellii morte interceptum absolvit G. Kroll, Berolini, 1928-1929.

Decretales D. Gregorii IX, una cum Glossis Restitutae, Romae, 1582.

Decretum Gratiani emendatum et notationibus illustratum, una cum glossis, Gregorii XIII Pont. Max. iussu editum, 2 vols., Romae 1582.

Jaffé, P., *Regesta Pontificum Romanorum ab condita Ecclesia ad annum post Christum natum MCXCVIII,* 2. ed., correctam et auctam auspiciis Gulielmi Wattenbach, curaverunt S. Lowenfeld, F. Kaltenbrunner, P. Ewald, 2 vols., Lipsiae, 1885-1888.

Liber Sextus Decretalium D. Bonifacii Papae VIII suae integritati una cum Clementinis et extravagantibus Earumque Glossis restitutus, Romae, 1582.

Mansi, Joannes, *Sacrorum Conciliorum Nova et Amplissima Collectio,* 53 vols. in 60, Parisiis, 1901-1927.

New Testament of Our Lord Jesus Christ, The, Confraternity Edition, Paterson, New Jersey: Saint Anthony's Guild Press, 1941.

Schroeder, H. J., *Canons and Decrees of the Council of Trent,* St. Louis: B. Herder Book Company, 1941.

Potthast, Augustus, *Regesta Pontificum Romanorum inde ab anno post Christum natum MCXCVIII ad annum MCCCIV,* 2 vols., Berolini, 1874-1875.

Quaranta, Stephanus, *Summa Bullarii Earumve Summorum Pontificum Constitutionum*, Venetiis, 1622.

Reference Works

Abbo, J. A.-Hannan, J. D., *The Sacred Canons*, 2 vols., St. Louis: B. Herder Book Company, 1952.

Altimarus, Blasius, *Tractatus de Nullitatibus in XVI Rubricis Divisus*, Neapoli, 1678.

Augustine, Charles, *A Commentary on the New Code of Canon Law*, 8 vols., Vol. VII, *Ecclesiastical Trails*, St. Louis: B. Herder Book Company, 1921.

Barbosa, Augustinus, *Collectanea Doctorum*, 6 vols. in 4, Romae, 1656.

Bartoccetti, V., *De Regulis Iuris Canonici*, Romae: Angelo Balardetti Editore, 1955.

Bassi, Franciscus, *Bibliotheca Iuris, Canonico-Civilis Practica*, 4 vols., Mutinae, 1757.

Bernardini, C., *Leges Processuales Vigentes apud S. Rotae Tribunal*, 2. ed., Romae, 1947.

Beste, U., *Introductio in Codicem*, 3. ed., Collegeville, Minn., 1946.

Blat, Albertus, *Commentarium Textus Codicis Iuris Canonici*, Liber IV, *De Processibus*, Romae: Collegio Angelico, 1927.

Bouix, D., *Tractatus de Judiciis Ecclesiasticis*, 2. ed., 2 vols., Parisiis, 1855.

Bouscaren, T. L.-Ellis, A. C., *Canon Law, A Text and Commentary*, 2. ed., Milwaukee: Bruce Publishing Company, 1951.

Camarda, Antonius, *Romanorum Pontificum Decretalium a Primo usque ad Sextum Librum Synopsis*, Romae, 1715.

Cappello, Felix, *Summa Iuris Canonici*, 3 vols., Vol. III, editio tertia emendata et aucta, Romae: Apud Aedes Universitatis Gregorianae, 1948.

Cocchi, Guidus, *Commentarium in Codicem Iuris Canonici*, 8 vols., Vol. I, 6. ed., 1947; Vol. II, 4. ed., 1937; Vol. IV, 4. ed., 1946; Vol. VII, 4. ed., 1938, Taurinorum Augustae: Marietti.

Connolly, Thomas A., *Appeals*, The Catholic University of America Canon Law Studies, n. 79, Washington, D.C.: The Catholic University of America, 1932.

Coronata, Matthaeus Conte a, *Institutiones Iuris Canonici*, 5 vols., Vol. III, *De Processibus*, 4. ed., Romae: Marietti, 1956.

De Angelis, Philippus, *Praelectiones Iuris Canonici*, 5 vols., Romae, 1877-1891.

De Bayso, Guido, *Rosarium seu in Decretarum Volumen Commentaria*, Venetiis, 1577.

De Luca, Joannes Baptista, *Theatrum Veritatis et Iustitiae*, 16 vols., Coloniae, 1706.

Devoti, Ioannes, *Institutionum Canonicarum Libri IV*, 4. ed., 4 vols. in 3, Venetiis, 1827.

Doheny, William J., *Canonical Procedure in Matrimonial Cases*, Vol. I, *Formal Judicial Procedure*, 2. ed., Milwaukee: The Bruce Publishing Company, 1948.

Dube, Arthur J., *The General Principles for the Reckoning of Time in Canon Law*, The Catholic University of America Canon Law Studies, n. 144, Washington, D.C.: The Catholic University of America Press, 1941.

Feeney, Thomas J., *Restitutio in Integrum*, The Catholic University of Canon Law Studies, n. 129, Washington, D.C.: The Catholic University of America Press, 1941.

Fermosinus, N. R., *Opera Omnia Canonica, Civilia et Criminalia*, 2. ed., 14 vols., Coloniae, 1741.

Ferreres, J., *Institutiones Canonicae*, 2. ed., 2 vols., Barcinone: Ex Typis Eugenii Subirana, 1920.

Galtier, F., *Code Oriental de Procédure Ecclésiastique*, Beyrouth, 1951.

Gasparri, P. Card., *Schema Codicis Iuris Canonici*, Lib. I, II (1912), III, V (1913), IV (1914), Romae: Typis Polyglottis Vaticanis.

Giménez Fernandez, Manuel, *Instituciones Juridicas en la Iglesia Catolica*, 2 vols., Saeta: Sociedad Anonima Española de Traductore y Autores, 1942.

Goyeneche, S., *De Processibus, Breves Adnotationes ad L. IV Codicis Iuris Canonici*, Vol. I in 2 pts., Romae: Ad S. Ioannis Lat., 1947.

Hanssen, Antonius, *De Sanctione Nullitatis in Processu Canonico*, Romae: Apollinaris, 1939.

Hostiensis, Cardinalis (Henricus de Segusio), *Commentaria in Quinque Decretalium Libros*, 5 vols., Venetiis, 1581.

Hurter, H., *Nomenclator literarius theologiae catholicae theologos exhibens aetate, natione, disciplinis distinctos*, 3. ed. emendata et aucta, 5 vols. in 6, Oeniponte: Libraria Academica Wagneriana, 1892-1899.

Jone, Heribert, *Commentarium in Codicem Iuris Canonici*, 3 vols., I (1950), II (1954), III (1955), Paderborn: Ferd. Schoeningh.

Jordanus, Pax, *Elucubrationes Diversae*, 3 vols., Coloniae, 1729.

Lauer, Arcturus, *Index Verborum Codicis Iuris Canonici*, Romae: Typis Polyglottis Vaticanus, 1941.

Lega, Michael, *Praelectiones in Textum Iuris Canonici de Iudiciis Ecclesiasticis in Scholis Pont. Sem. Rom. Habitae*, 4 vols., Romae, 1896-1901.

———,-Bartoccetti, V., *Commentarius in Iudicia Ecclesiastica iuxta Codicem Iuris Canonici*, 3 vols., Romae: Anonima Libraria Cattolica Italiana, 1938-1941.

Maranta, Robertus, *Speculum Aureum et Lumen Advocatorum Praxis Civilis*, Venetiis, 1590.

Marchesi, Franciscus, *Summula Iuris Canonici ad Usum Scholarum*, 4 vols., Vol. III, *De Processibus*, Albae Pompeiae (Italia): Editiones Paulinae, 1953.

Maschat, Remigius, *Institutiones Canonicae*, 2 vols., Romae, 1757.

Michiels, G., *Normae Generales Iuris Canonici*, 2. ed., 2 vols., Parisiis-Tornaci-Romae: Desclée et Socii, 1949.

Migne, J. P., *Patrologiae Cursus Completus, Series Latina*, 221 vols., Parisiis, 1844-1855.

Noone, John J., *Nullity in Judicial Acts*, The Catholic University of America Canon Law Studies, n. 297, Washington, D.C.: The Catholic University of America Press, 1950.

Noval, J., *Commentarium Codicis Iuris Canonici*, Lib. IV, *De Processibus*, Pars I, *De Iudiciis*, Augustae Taurinorum: Marietti, 1920.

Ottaviani, Alaphridus, *Institutiones Iuris Publici Ecclesiastici*, 3. ed., 2 vols., Civitate Vaticana: Typis Polyglottis Vaticanis, 1947-1948.

Panormitanus (Nicholas de Tudeschis), *Commentaria in Quinque Libros Decretalium*, 5 vols. in 7, Venetiis, 1588.

Passerinus, P. M., *Commentaria in Sextum Librum Decretalium*, 5 vols. in 2, Venetiis, 1698.

Pellegrini, Carolus, *Praxis Vicariorum et Omnium in Utroque Foro Iusdicentium*, Venetiis, 1696.

Pierantonelli, Pacificus, *Praxis Fori Ecclesiastici*, Romae, 1883.

Pinna, Giovanni, *Praxis Iudicialis Canonica*, Romae: Officium Libri Catholici, 1952.

Pirhing, E., *Ius Canonicum in V Libros Decretalium*, ed. novissima, 4 vols., Dilingae, 1722.

Regatillo, Edwardus, *Institutiones Iuris Canonici*, 2 vols., Santander: Sal Terrae, 1942.

Reiffenstuel, Anacletus, *Ius Canonicum Universum*, 7 vols., Parisiis, 1864-1882.

Roberti, Franciscus, *Codicis Iuris Canonici Schemata*, Lib. IV, *De Processibus*, Romae: Typis Polyglottis Vaticanis, 1940.

———, *De Processibus*, 2 vols., Romae: Apud Aedes Facultates Iuridicae ad S. Apollinaris, 1926.

———, *De Processibus*, Vol. I, 4. ed., Romae: Apud Custodiam Librariam Pontificii Instituti Utriusque Iuris, 1956.

Rocca, Fernando, *Istituzioni di Diritto Processuale Canonico*, Torino, 1946

Roelker, Edward, *Invalidating Laws*, Paterson, N.J.: St. Anthony Guild Press, 1955.

Rufinus, *Die* SUMMA DECRETORUM *des Magister Rufinus*, ed. Heinrich Singer, Paderborn, 1902.

Santamaria, Peña F., *Comentarios al Código Canónico*, 6 vols., Madrid, 1919-1922.

Santi, Franciscus, *Praelectiones Iuris Canonici*, 4. ed., curante M. Leitner, 5 vols., Ratisbonae, 1903-1905.

Scaccia, Sigismundus, *Tractatus de Appellationibus*, 3. ed., Coloniae, 1717.

Schmalzgrueber, Franciscus, *Ius Ecclesiasticum Universum*, 5 vols. in 12, Romae, 1843-1845.

Schulte, Johann F. von, *Die Geschichte der Quellen und Literatur des canonischen Rechts von Gratian bis auf die Gegenwart*, 3 vols. in 2, Stuttgart, 1875-1880.

Sipos, Stephanus, *Enchiridion Iuris Canonici*, Pécs: Ex Typographia "Haladas R.T.", 1926.

Stephanus Tornacensis, *Die* SUMMA *des Stephanus Tornacensis über das* DECRETUM *Gratiani*, ed. J. F. von Schaulte, Giessen, 1891.

Stickler, A. M., *Historia Iuris Canonici Latini*, I, *Historia Fontium*, Augustae Taurinorum: Apud Custodiam Librariam Pontif. Athenaei Salesiani, 1950.

Torquebiau, P., Naz, R., De Clercq, C., Jombart, E., *Traité de Droit Canonique*, 4 vols., Vol. IV, Des Procès, Des Délits, Des Peines, Letouzey et Ané, 1949.

Torre, J., *Processus Matrimonialis*, 3. ed., M. D'Auria, Pontificius Editor, Neapoli (Italia), 1956.

Tuschus, Cardinalis, *Practicae Conclusiones Iuris, in Omni Foro Frequentiores*, 7 vols., I vol. Supple., Lugduni, 1634.

Van Espen, Z. B., *Ius Ecclesiasticum Universum*, 10 vols., Venetiis, 1769.

Van Hove, A., *Commentarium Lovaniense in Codicem Iuris Canonici, Prolegomena ad Codicem Iuris Canonici*, 2. ed., Mechliniae-Romae: H. Dessain, 1945.

Vermeersch, A.-Creusen, J., *Epitome Iuris Canonici*, 3 vols., Vol. II, 7. ed., Mechiniae-Romae: H. Dessain, 1954.

Wenger, Leopold, *Institutes of the Roman Law of Civil Procedure*, Revised ed., New York: Veritas Press, 1940.

Wernz, Franciscus X., *Ius Decretalium*, 6 vols., Vols. I-IV, 2. ed., Romae et Prati, 1905-1912.

———,-Vidal, P., *Ius Canonicum*, 7 vols. in 8, Vol. V, 3. ed., 1946, Vol. VI, *De Processibus*, 2. ed., 1949, Romae: Apud Aedes Universitatis Gregorianae, 1949.

Woywod, S., *A Practical Commentary on the Code of Canon Law*, Revised and enlarged edition by Callistus Smith, 2 vols., New York: Joseph F. Wagner, Inc., 1948.

Articles

Ciprotti, P., "De novis probationibus post conclusionem in causa," *Apollinaris*, XII (1939), 110-116.

Hanssen, A., "De sanctione nullitatis in processu canonico," *Apollinaris*, XI (1938), 71-109; 215-263; 381-403; XII (1939), 198-251.

Roberti, F., "Circa limites querelae nullitatis et restitutionis in integrum," *Apollinaris*, I (1928), 476-483.

———, "De nullitate sententiae," *Apollinaris*, II (1929), 76-78.

PERIODAL

Apollinaris, Romae, 1928—.

ABBREVIATIONS

AAS—*Acta Apostolicae Sedis.*
c.—canon seu caput (iuris antiqui).
C.I.C.—Codex Iuris Canonici.
D.—Digesta.
Fontes—*Codicis Iuris Canonici Fontes.*
R.J.—Regula Iuris.
S.C.C.—Sacra Congregatio Concilii.
S.C. de Sacramentis—Sacra Congregatio de disciplina Sacramentorum.
S.R.R.—Sarca Romana Rota.

BIOGRAPHICAL NOTE

JOHN P. DUNNIVAN was born in Olpe, Kansas, on June 12, 1928. His early education was received in the public schools of Garnett, Kansas. He attended St. Benedict's College in Atchison, Kansas, graduating from that institution in May, 1949, with a degree of Bachelor of Arts. In September, 1949, he entered Kenrick Seminary at St. Louis, Missouri. Having been ordained to the priesthood on February 28, 1953, by His Excellency, the Most Reverend Edward J. Hunkeler, D.D., LL.D., Archbishop of Kansas City in Kansas, he was engaged in parochial work until September, 1954. He then entered the School of Canon Law of the Catholic University of America, Washington, D.C., in October, 1954. He received the degree of the Baccalaureate in Canon Law in June, 1955, and the degree of the Licentiate in Canon Law in June, 1956.

APHABETICAL INDEX

INDEX OF CANONS

CANON LAW STUDIES*

375. Kelleher, Rev. Francis T., A.B., J.C.L., Judicial expenses.
376. Bantigue, Rev. Pedro N., J.C.L., The Provincial council of Manila of 1771. (Its text followed by a commentary on *Actio* II, *De Episcopis*)
377. Burns, Rev. Dennis J., J.C.L., Matrimonal indissolubility: contrary conditions.
378. Deutsch, Rev. Bernard F., J.C.L., Jurisdiction of pastors in the external forum.
379. Dunnivan, Rev. John P., A.B., J.C.L., Prejudicial Attempts in pending litigation.
380. Ernst, Rev. Albert C., A.B., J.C.L., Free admission to church for sacred rites.
381. Frattin, Mr. Peter Louis, J.C.L., The matrimonial impediment of impotence: occlusion of the spermatic ducts and vaginismus.
382. Henry, Rev. Charles W., O.S.B., A.B., S.T.L., J.C.L., Canonical relations between bishops and abbots at the beginning of the tenth century.
383. Hoffman, Rev. Lawrence J., A.B., J.C.L., Clergy conference: Canon 131.
384. Markham, Rev. James J., A.B., S.T.L., J.C.L., The Sacred Congregation of Seminaries and Universities of Studies.
385. McGrath, Rev. John J., A.B., LL.B., J.C.L., A comparative study of crime and its imputability in ecclesiastical criminal law and in American criminal law.
386. McGuire, Rev. James D., O.R.S.A., J.C.L., The postulancy.
387. Munday, Rev. James E., J.C.L., Ecclesiastical Property in Australia and New Zealand.
388. Murphy, Rev. Joseph P., A.B., J.C.L., The laws of the State of New York affecting church property.
389. Pickard, Rev. William M., J.C.L., Judicial experts: a source of evidence in ecclesiastical trials.
390. Ruddy, Rev. James, J.C.L., The Apostolic Constitution *Christus Dominus:* text, translation and commentary, with short annotations on the Motu Proprio *Sacram Communionem.*
391. Vanyo, Rev. Leo V., A.B., J.C.L., Requisites of intention in the reception of the sacraments.

* For a complete list of the available numbers of this series apply to the Catholic University of America Press, 620 Michigan Avenue, N.E., Washington (17), D.C., for a general catalogue.

www.ingramcontent.com/pod-product-compliance
Lightning Source LLC
LaVergne TN
LVHW050229080826
844660LV00012B/503

* 9 7 8 0 8 1 3 2 2 5 3 9 5 *